Those Who Wait

To: My Daughter
Teyulla
With Love,
From: Mother
Peggy.

Those Who Wait

Learning How to Wait on the Lord in an Impatient World

Rosemary McKnight

GOSPEL ADVOCATE CO.
P.O.Box 150
Nashville, TN. 37202

THOSE WHO WAIT

Published by the Gospel Advocate Co.
P.O. Box 150, Nashville, TN 37202

ISBN 89225-365-7

This book is dedicated to
David and Debbie Bright and
Jeff and Mary Alice Trotter,
two couples who know what it
means to wait on the Lord.
They have been a great encouragement
to our family throughout our times of waiting.

Contents

Foreword

At the conclusion of each chapter are sections designated as *Sharing Session* and *Action Guide*. The thoughts and comments suggested in the *Sharing Session* are to be used at the beginning of each class to get the class members to participate and to promote discussion throughout the class. It will also help class members get to know one another better.

The *Action Guide* is a practical application of something taught in the lesson. It is designed to help participants continue to think about the lesson outside of class and apply what they have learned.

Introduction

"They that wait upon the Lord shall
renew their strength;
they shall mount up with wings as eagles;
they shall run, and not be weary;
and they shall walk, and not faint."
Isaiah 40:31 (KJV)

Isaiah 40:31 has been one of my favorite passages of Scripture for years. I first learned the verse through a song, "Teach Me Lord to Wait." I used to love to sing the part, "They shall mount up on wings like eagles." It sounded so glorious.

It was ten years later that I had to back up and learn the meaning of the beginning of Isaiah 40:31—the part about waiting on the Lord. What a difficult lesson!

One spring day my husband Gary came home from work early to tell me he had lost his job. No reason was given. That was four years ago. We still don't know why he was asked to resign. In the months that followed, Gary diligently searched for a job in his field of work, but he found nothing. Time came for us to move out of the house. Where would we go? We did not know when, where or if Gary would find employment.

My parents offered to let us move in with them. It seemed we had no other option at the time; so we loaded up a truck, put all of our things in storage, and moved in with my parents. After ten years of living away, it was difficult to swallow our pride and come home.

I remember Gary saying, "Give me two weeks; I'll have a job, and we'll be on our own again." But two weeks turned into two months, and still there was no employment.

Losing a job and not being able to support his family are critical blows to any man. So much of a man's self-esteem is based on his feelings toward his work and his ability to provide for his wife and children. These months of unemployment were so difficult for all of us, but especially for Gary.

Gary was finally able to get part-time work selling men's clothing in a department store during the Christmas season. He was kept on after the holidays, but the salary was not enough to support our family. So, we continued to live with my parents. During this time Gary began to take some classes at Memphis State University.

Many times we asked, "Why has this happened to us? What is the purpose in this? Where is God leading us? When will our waiting be over?" I cannot remember a more stressful or discouraging time in our marriage.

During this time I received a letter from a dear friend who lived in the town from which we had moved. She said, "Rosemary, I know you are discouraged, but you are going to grow a lot from this experience. Someday you may even write a book about waiting upon the Lord because you can share with others what it means to wait." She also sent a framed picture with the words of Isaiah 40:31 printed on it.

Gary and I hung that picture in our bedroom. The words of Isaiah 40:31 began to strengthen and sustain us. We did not know why we were having to wait or exactly what we were waiting for, but the words continually reminded us that God would renew our strength and help us persevere.

It was that letter and picture that inspired this study. Today eight additional pictures containing the words of Isaiah 40:31 also hang on our bedroom wall. Gary and I are still waiting, but we are now able to look back and see many blessings that have come from our waiting experience. My friend was right. We have grown a lot during these years of waiting.

Gary and I feel as if the end is in sight regarding our wait. Because Gary was unable to find employment in his field of work, he made the decision to go back to school and take courses in a different area of study. He has completed the coursework toward a doctorate in education and is writing his dissertation. Had we not been placed in "God's waiting room," Gary might never have pursued this degree. We feel these past four years of waiting have been a time of preparation and growth.

We continue to live with my parents. People ask, "How can you all live together and get along so well?" It has required extra patience on the part of all, but, oh, what a bond has been established—especially between our two young sons and their grandparents! And how thankful we were that we were living here when my mother fell and broke her hip last year. God has packed so many blessings into these four years of waiting.

I will be the first to admit I don't understand God's timing or why He sometimes asks His children to wait, but I believe with all my heart that God knows what is best. It is my prayer that as you read and study this material your faith in God will grow as you wait upon the Lord and that, in turn, you will help and strengthen others who are waiting.

1

What Are *You* Waiting For?

Here we are you and I
sitting in God's waiting room—again.
He didn't answer our petition
with a yes, no, perhaps or maybe.
But He said, "Wait here!"
So here we are you and I
sitting in God's waiting room—
In yet another holding pattern.[1]
—Joyce Landorf

The words in the poem above were on the front of a card that Gary and I received soon after Gary lost his job and we moved in with my parents. Gary's college roommate and his wife sent the card to encourage us. Inside were the words, "We wait with you!" and the following verse: "Wait for the Lord, He will come and save you! Be brave, stouthearted and courageous. Yes, wait and He will help you" (Psalm 27:14).

We reflected on a time when these dear friends had also been in God's waiting room. We knew they understood what it meant to wait. Their love and concern at this time was a great encouragement to us.

As we examined our friendships and began to look at others about us, we realized we were not alone in God's waiting room. It seemed almost everyone was waiting for something. If they were not presently waiting, most of them had been in God's waiting room at some point in their lives.

Types of Waiting

People like to think they can plan ahead and order their lives. We set goals and begin to strive to achieve those goals. Often our plans and goals are put on hold, and we enter a time of waiting. We realize how little control we have on the timetable of our lives. Our timetable is really in God's hands.

Let's examine some areas in our lives in which we may be required to wait.

1. Physical Waiting. We all can immediately think of those who are waiting physically. We see those about us who are faced with a terminal illness who are waiting, hoping and praying for a cure. There are those who are undergoing treatment who must wait to see if the treatment will be effective. We know of others who live in constant pain who are waiting for release from that pain. There are those who have been injured or required surgery, and they must wait to resume their normal activities until their recovery is complete. Many couples are waiting as Hannah and Elkanah waited, hoping and praying that they will conceive a child.

Our family learned about physical waiting this year when my mother fell and broke her hip. Broken bones don't heal quickly. There was surgery, a hospital stay, therapy, months of gradual progress from a walker to a cane, and then, finally, walking alone. Physical waiting cannot be rushed.

When we are waiting physically, we must remember God's awareness of our needs and His compassion. We also must remember we have a savior who also suffered physical pain. He understands. He cares. "Yet the Lord longs to be gracious to you; He rises to show you compassion. For the Lord is a God of justice. Blessed are all who wait for him" (Isaiah 30:18).

2. Emotional Waiting. Emotional waiting is often more difficult than physical waiting. Often we wait alone, afraid to express our hurting emotions to others. Christians may find it difficult to help those who are waiting emotionally simply because they are not aware of how they can help. They want to help, but they are afraid they will say the wrong thing. So they do nothing.

Emotional waiting includes those who are grieving over the death of a loved one. They wait and wonder if the emptiness and grief will ever subside. It includes those experiencing marital problems or problems with other family members (parents, siblings, children). They wonder if things will ever get better.

Emotional waiting also involves those who have been through a divorce. They are waiting for the hurt to heal and also trying to adjust to being single again or being a single parent. Emotional waiting involves the lonely—the shut-ins, the newcomers, the widows, the singles, and those who find it difficult to make friends. They wait for a visit, a phone call, a letter or a friend.

Unemployment and financial stress are emotional waiting periods. People in these situations may feel embarrassed, and they are reluctant to share their emotions for fear others will judge them harshly. The introduction to this book describes our situation when Gary unexpectedly lost his job. I remember how it shattered Gary's confidence in himself.

There is no set timetable for emotional healing. Every person must face each new day and say, as the psalmist David said, "I wait for you, O Lord; You will answer, O Lord my God" (Psalm 38:15).

3. Spiritual Waiting. Is there a loved one for whom you have prayed for many years? Perhaps you studied God's Word with this special person, but he or she never obeyed the gospel. Maybe it is your

"Wait for the Lord, He will come and save you! Be brave, stouthearted and courageous. Yes, wait and He will help you" (Psalm 27:14).

spouse, your child, a parent, or a very special friend. The desire of your heart is to see this person become a Christian. You are waiting in a spiritual waiting room.

There is a lady in our congregation who prayed for years that her husband would become a Christian. She waited year after year. He would come with her to services but never obeyed the gospel. She continued to pray and remained strong and faithful. Finally, when her husband was over 60 years of age, he was baptized into Christ and now is very active in the Lord's church. Since then she has seen her daughter-in-law become a Christian too. This Christian sister knows what it means to wait spiritually. Her faithfulness throughout her years of waiting were not in vain.

You may be like the father of the prodigal son. You are waiting for a loved one to come back to the church. You ache when you see sin in lives of those you love; yet, you know you cannot repent for them. You must wait for them to change and come back to God.

Spiritual waiting may be a personal struggle as we wait for growth in the Lord. Growth is often painful. It takes time to deal with the sins in our lives and to develop the characteristics God desires His children to have.

Ultimately, all Christians are waiting for Christ's return. We long for that home in heaven when we can live with God eternally. We wait for a time when there are no more tears, pain, death or sorrow. As we wait, we utter the prayer the apostle John recorded in Revelation 22:20 when Jesus said, "Yes, I am coming soon." John replied, "Amen. Come, Lord Jesus." That is spiritual waiting. ". . . We wait eagerly for our adoption as sons, the redemption of our bodies. . . . But if we hope for what we do not yet have, we wait for it patiently" (Romans 8:23,25).

We Wait with You

I don't know for what you are waiting. You may have waited for an answer to a prayer for so long you think you can't wait any longer. Don't give up! You're not in God's waiting room alone. There are those who can say to you, as our friends said to us in the card they sent, "We wait with you!"

God does hear your prayers. When God does not immediately respond to the cries of His children, it is because He wants to accomplish some gracious purpose in their lives.

We may not always understand God's timing. We may question why and rebel at the idea of waiting.

After all, we live in an "instant society." But God's timing is best. Isaiah wrote, " 'For my thoughts are not your thoughts, neither are your ways my ways,' declares the Lord. 'As the heavens are higher than the earth, so are my ways higher than your ways and my thoughts than your thoughts' " (Isaiah 55:8,9).

God sees the total picture. We see only the here and now. His thoughts and ways are higher than our own. He is divine, and we are only human. His plans are better than our plans. We were not meant to understand everything that happens on this earth, but we must have enough faith to accept that God knows what is best, and He is working for our good.

The following story has been a great encouragement to me as I have waited. This beautiful story illustrates how God's will is better than our own. I hope it will encourage you as you wait upon the Lord.

God's Trees

Far away, on a hillside, grew a forest of trees. The trees were very happy with life just as it was. But sometimes they spoke of the future, of things they would like to do and be when they grew up.

In this forest there was a mother tree and her three little trees. One tree said, "I should like to be a baby's cradle. I think a baby is the sweetest thing I have ever seen, and I should like to be made into a baby's bed."

A second tree spoke. "That would not please me at all. I want to be something important. I should like to be a great ship, strong and stately. I should like to cross many waters and carry cargoes of gold."

A third little tree stood off by himself and did not speak. "What would you like to be?" asked Mother Tree. "Have you no dreams for the future?"

"No dream," he answered, "except to stand on this hillside and point men to God. What could a tree do better than that?"

Years passed, and the little trees grew tall and beautiful. One day men came to the forest and cut down the first tree. "I wonder whether I shall be made into a baby's cradle now," he thought. But the little tree was not made into a cradle. Instead, it was hewn into rough pieces and carelessly put together to form a manger in a stable in Bethlehem. He was heartbroken. "This is not what I planned," he wailed, "to have cattle eating out of me."

But God, who loves little trees, whispered to him, "Wait. I will show you something." And He did! For on a cold, still night, Mary and Joseph came to that stable and there she gave birth to the son of God—Jesus—and laid Him in that manger. "This is wonderful," whispered the tree. "In all my dreams I never thought to hold a baby like this. This *is* better than all my planning. I'm part of a miracle."

Months passed, and men came again to the forest to cut down the second tree. "I wonder whether I shall be made into a great vessel now and do great things," he thought. But instead he became a tiny fishing boat, owned by a simple Galilean fisherman named Peter. The little boat was most unhappy. "To think that my life has come to this. Just a smelly fishing boat. And Peter not a very good fisherman!"

But God, who loves little trees, said to him, "Wait. I will show you something." And He did. One day, from out of the crowd, came a person named Jesus. He sat in the boat and taught the crowd beautiful words of wisdom. Then He told Peter to launch out into the deep and let his nets down. There were so many fish that the net broke. The little boat trembled, not so much from the weight of the fish as with the weight of wonder in his heart. "In all my dreams I never thought to carry a cargo like this! Why, I'm part of a miracle. This *is* better than all my planning."

Weeks went by and one day men came to the forest to cut down the third tree, the one who wanted to just stand on a hill and point men to God. He was most unhappy as the axe cut into his bark. "I don't want to go into the valley," he cried. "Why couldn't men leave me alone!" The men tore away the branches and cut deeper into his very heart. They hewed it apart, then put it together in the form of a rude cross. "This is terrible. They are going to kill someone on me. I never wanted this to happen; I only wanted to point men to God," he wailed.

But God, who loves little trees, said to him, "Wait. I will show you something." And He did. A few days later, a great multitude gathered outside Jerusalem. In their midst was Jesus, carrying the cross. When they came to the place called Calvary, they nailed Him to that cross and crucified Him. The cross shuddered beneath the weight of agony and shame. But then a miracle happened.

Jesus, when He had cried with a loud voice, gave up His life. And the earth quaked and the rocks trembled. When the centurion saw these things, he was afraid and said, "Truly this man was the Son of God."

Then the little tree that had become a cross remembered the echo of a past promise from heaven: "And I, if I be lifted up from the earth, will draw all men unto Me." The tree began to understand: "This is wonderful," he thought. "I'm part of a miracle. In all my dreams I never thought to point men to God in this way. This *is* better than all my planning." And so it was. For hundreds of trees stood on the hill slopes through the years, but not one of them has reconciled men to God.[2]

[1]Landorf, Joyce. "God's Waiting Room." Used by permission of Day-Spring Cards. Siloam Springs, AR: Outreach Publications.

[2]*God's Trees.* Used by permission of Child Evangelism Fellowship, Inc., Warrenton, Missouri 63383.

Sharing Session: What are you waiting for? All members of the class may tell something they are waiting for or tell about a time when they had to wait for something in the past.

Action Guide: Memorize Isaiah 40:31.

For Thought and Discussion

1. Bring a newspaper to class. Notice how many articles involve some sort of waiting.
2. Divide the class into three groups. Let each group take one of the types of waiting: physical, emotional, or spiritual. Discuss that section of this chapter, and share your thoughts with the class.
3. What is the ultimate end of the Christian's waiting? Read Revelation 22:20. Do you think Christians have this attitude?
4. Why do you think God requires us to wait?
5. What are some petty things (such as red lights) we wait on each day? How does this waiting differ from the types of waiting discussed in this chapter?
6. Pray specifically about your waiting experience. Ask God for patience and increased faith as you wait. Pray for others you know who are also waiting.
7. Why is it so difficult to wait?
8. Ask someone to read the story of *God's Trees* aloud to the class. Discuss how God's will is better than all our planning.

2

Isaiah 40— A Context Study

The theme of this book is based on Isaiah 40:31, "But those who hope in the Lord will renew their strength. They will soar on wings like eagles: they will run and not grow weary; they shall walk and not be faint." In this chapter we will study why this verse was written.

As Christians study the Bible, it is important that we look at the context of the passage we are studying. All too often verses are pulled out of context, and they are misinterpreted or misused. When we study a specific passage, we need to ask such questions as these: To whom was this written? What do the verses before and after this passage teach? Does this passage fit in with an overall theme? Why was it written? After we answer these questions, we can focus on what the passage means to us today.

This chapter will be a study of the context of Isaiah 40:31. We will look at the entire fortieth chapter of Isaiah and see what Isaiah was teaching. The following chapters of this book will deal more specifically with verse 31. Hopefully, as you read, study and pray, you will gain a better understanding of what it means to wait upon the Lord.

Who Was Isaiah?

Isaiah was the writer of this great passage. What do we know about him? Isaiah is regarded as the greatest of the Old Testament prophets. A prophet was a messenger of God. The messages of the prophets sometimes told about the time in which they were living, and they sometimes foretold the future. Isaiah did both.

Isaiah prophesied to the nation of Judah during the divided kingdom. He is referred to as the "king's prophet." Isaiah prophesied during the reigns of four kings—Uzziah, Jotham, Ahaz and Hezekiah. Only one of these kings, Hezekiah, demonstrated love and respect for God (Isaiah 36-39). Unlike many of the prophets, Isaiah spoke directly to the kings.

Isaiah was also known as the "messianic prophet." Ten different passages in the book of Isaiah refer to Christ, the Messiah. You may wish to read Isaiah 53 as an example of Isaiah's messianic prophecy.

We learn something of Isaiah's attitude toward serving God in the sixth chapter of Isaiah. In verse eight the Lord asked, "Whom shall I send? And who will go for us?" Isaiah immediately replied, "Here am I. Send me!" Perhaps it was Isaiah's willingness to go, his eagerness to serve God, that truly made him the greatest of the prophets. We must ask ourselves if we have that same willingness to serve God.

The Book of Isaiah

The book of Isaiah was written to the nation of Judah—God's chosen people. It is divided into two sections. The first section, Chapters 1–39, refers to events leading up to the captivity of the nation. These chapters contain exhortations and warnings of divine judgment and writings about the sins and misery of the people. They also contain prophecies about the surrounding nations. Isaiah was preparing the people for what was about to happen. The Babylonians were going to destroy Jerusalem and take the people of Judah back to Babylon as captives.

The second section, Chapters 40–66, contains predictions, warnings and promises that refer to events beyond the captivity and reach down through the centuries to the Christian dispensation. This part is especially rich in messianic prophecies.

As you read the book of Isaiah, it is helpful to understand if the passage refers to a time before or after the captivity. Let us look specifically at Isaiah 40.

Isaiah 40

Isaiah 39 tells of Isaiah's informing King Hezekiah that the Babylonians would come and carry off everything in his palace. He adds that even Hezekiah's descendants would serve as eunuchs in the palace of Babylon. History proved this to be true. The nation of Judah was carried into captivity by Nebuchadnezzar, king of Babylon (2 Kings 25). These Jews walked about 600 miles to serve the people of Babylon. Only the sick and lame were allowed to stay in Jerusalem. The city was destroyed.

The Jews remained in captivity for 70 years before they were allowed to return to Jerusalem. Isaiah 40 was written to comfort those Jews and to give them hope as they looked forward to their return. Isaiah is writing to people who knew what it meant to wait upon the Lord. They had waited 70 years for release from their captivity. They were homesick and fainthearted. What does Isaiah tell them?

A message of comfort and a promise of deliverance are given in verses 1-5. Isaiah begins by saying, "Comfort, comfort my people." God had not forsaken them. He was aware of their hurting and homesickness. Isaiah adds that a harbinger would go ahead of the people to prepare the way for their return (verses 3-5). It was the harbinger's duty to open passages, level the way, and remove impediments so the 600-mile trip on foot would be easier for those who would return.

The sixth verse refers to a different voice. In this section (verses 6-10), the voice urges the Jews not to dwell on earthly, temporal things but to focus on spiritual, eternal things. He reminds them, "The grass withers and the flowers fall, but the word of our God stands forever" (verse 8).

Verses 12-20 teach the insignificance of man. It would have been easy for the Jews to return to Jerusalem and forget about God. They must have dreamed of rebuilding a great nation once again and crowning a powerful king. God wanted to remind them before their return that true deliverance comes from God. No nation can begin to compare with God.

The last section of Isaiah 40, verses 21-31, was written to remind the Jews of the power of God. Isaiah refers to God's power in nature (verse 26) and God's power to know and understand us (verses 27,28). He tells them God's power is eternal (verse 28). Finally, he encourages these homesick Jews by telling them God will give them the power and strength they need for the long trip home.

Verses 28-31 are the climax of this beautiful chapter of comfort and hope:

Do you not know? Have you not heard? The Lord is the everlasting God, the Creator of the ends of the earth. He will not grow tired or weary, and his understanding no one can fathom. He gives strength to the weary and increases the power of the weak.

Even youths grow tired and weary, and young men stumble and fall; but those who hope in the Lord will renew their strength. They will soar on wings like eagles; they will run and not grow weary, they will walk and not be faint.

What About Me?

We have discussed what this chapter meant to the Jews in captivity. Now, what does it say to us today? What can we learn from Isaiah 40 that will help us as we wait upon the Lord? I believe there are five key verses in this chapter that will help us as we wait. I would encourage you to underline them in your Bible.

1. *"Comfort, comfort my people, says your God"* (verse 1).

What a consolation to those who wait to realize true comfort comes from God! God is referred to as the "Father of compassion" and the "God of all comfort" in 2 Corinthians 1:3. God cares. He knows when we are hurting and discouraged. He understands, and He offers us comfort.

There are times when we wait and feel as if no one understands. Nothing anyone does makes us feel better. If we can only hear these words, "Comfort, comfort my people," perhaps our hope can be renewed.

2. *"The grass withers and the flowers fall, but the word of God stands forever"* (verse 8).

How does God comfort us? He is not here to literally put His arms around us or talk to us. He comforts us through His Word, and we know His Word will never fail.

Does it really work? I remember a time when Gary and I were waiting on the Lord. We lost our first baby in a miscarriage. We wondered if God would give us a child. A friend wrote a letter and included in it the words to Psalm 20. It begins, "May the Lord answer you when you are in distress; may the name of the God of Jacob protect you." What comfort was in the words of that Psalm! I remember crying as I read it. I have read it many times since then and encouraged others to read it when they were discouraged.

God's Word, the Bible, never fails. Comfort is there if only we will spend time reading and studying His Word.

3. *"He tends his flock like a shepherd: He gathers the lambs in his arms and carries them close to his heart; he gently leads those that have young"* (Isaiah 40:11).

What a special relationship exists between a shepherd and his sheep. This is so beautifully illustrated in the parable of the lost sheep (Luke 15). Although the shepherd had 99 other sheep, he left them to go and search for the one that was lost. When he found that sheep, he put it on his shoulders and brought it home, and there was great rejoicing. Each sheep is special to its shepherd.

John 10 describes Jesus as the good shepherd. Jesus says, "I know my sheep and my sheep know me . . . and I lay down my life for the sheep" (John 10:14). Notice it said, "I *know* my sheep." Jesus does know us, and He carries us close to His heart. What comfort it is to the Christian to be able to say, "The Lord is my Shepherd."

We were discussing Isaiah 40:11 in our ladies' class one evening. A mother of four children said the part of this verse that meant so much to her was the ending, "he gently leads those that have young." She expressed a belief that God must have a special awareness of mothers who are attempting to teach their children the Bible. The verse encourages her as she raises four children. She likes His gentle leading.

4. *"Lift up your eyes and look to the heavens: Who created all these? He who brings out the starry host one by one, and calls them each by name. Because of his great power and mighty strength, not one of them is missing"* (verse 26).

In our waiting, Christians can draw strength from God's creation. There are so many things in nature that remind us of God's power and love. In this verse, Isaiah tells the Jews to look up at the stars. Jesus used many examples from nature as He taught—the birds, the lilies of the field, a storm, a farmer sowing seed, a pearl, fish, and many others.

Each change of season and its unique beauty tells us of God's design. He provides both sunshine and rain, knowing we need both. The beauty of mountains and the sound of the ocean on the beach help many to relax and feel a release of tension.

David expressed it this way, "I lift up my eyes to the hills—where does my help come from? My help comes from the Lord, the Maker of heaven and earth" (Psalm 121:1,2). God's creation can remind us of his care. If we will just lift up our eyes, we will be strengthened.

5. *". . . He will not grow tired or weary, and his understanding no one can fathom. He gives strength to the weary and increases the power of the weak"* (Isaiah 40:28b,29).

Isn't it wonderful to know God never grows tired or weary? That means a lot to me because when I am tired, I grow weary. Then I tend to make mountains out of molehills. Problems seem so much worse when I am tired.

There was an elder of the church we attended in Tuscaloosa, Alabama, who used to give good advice. When people were faced with a problem or an important decision, he would tell them, "Go home and sleep on it. In the morning the problem may not seem so great, or the decision may be easier to make." He knew people don't always make the best decisions when they are tired, and problems may seem much worse than they actually are. Sometimes what we need most is a good night's sleep. But God *never* grows tired or weary! He has an inexhaustible supply of strength and power, and He will give it to those who are weary and weak.

To those who are weary from waiting on the Lord and weak from physical exhaustion, don't give up! God will give you strength and power. He will comfort you and sustain you. *The Pulpit Commentary* says, "God has varied ways of relieving our weakness and restoring our strength. But whatever the instrumentality, it is God that does it, God's Spirit that fills it. . . . We may be maimed, bruised, broken, but God can lift us up." Keep waiting. Keep hoping. Keep enduring. Keep trusting in God. Why? Because ". . . those who [wait] upon the Lord will renew their strength. They will soar on wings like eagles; they will run and not grow weary; they will walk and not be faint."

Sharing Session: Isaiah 40:26 reminds us to look to the heavens and be reminded of God's power and strength. What is something in nature that helps you feel close to God or reminds you of His power?

Action Guide: Read Isaiah 40 every day for one week. If possible, read it from different versions of the Bible.

For Thought and Discussion

1. What are some scriptures that comfort you? Share them in class.
2. Find some additional facts about Isaiah the prophet. Read what some commentaries say about Isaiah 40. Share these comments in class.
3. Divide the class into five groups. Have each group discuss one of the key verses mentioned in the section "What About Me?" Share the discussion with the class.
4. Name some evidences of God's power.
5. Why is it important to study the context of a passage of scripture? How do we learn about the context? Can you think of examples of verses that have been misused because they were quoted out of context?
6. The Jews were homesick and waiting to return to Jerusalem. Compare this to Christians being homesick for heaven.
7. How does our physical well-being affect the way we handle problems? Share some ways you handle problems when you are tired.
8. The following verses from Isaiah 40 are also mentioned in the New Testament: Isaiah 40:3 in Mark 1:3; Isaiah 40:6-8 in 1 Peter 1:24,25; Isaiah 40:11 in John 10:11-16; Isaiah 40:13,28 in Romans 11:33-36. Look up these verses and discuss the context in which they are used to help New Testament Christians.
9. Do some research on the Babylonian Captivity and report it to the class. Then pretend you are a captive, and do one of the following activities:

—Write a letter to a loved one who remained in Jerusalem.
—Make a diary of what it would be like to be a captive.
—Role play some conversations of the captives as they anticipate their return.
—Make up a song to sing as you make the journey back to Jerusalem.

3

Renewing Our Strength

"They that wait upon the Lord shall renew their strength . . ." (KJV).

Have you ever waited so long for something that you were ready to give up? You felt exhausted from the wait—physically, mentally, emotionally and spiritually. You began to feel the waiting would never end, and a feeling of panic set in. The panic made you feel as if you had to do something to change things, and you had to do it *now!* You just could not stand to wait any longer.

That is exactly how Sarah felt. She had waited and waited for a child. Genesis 16 tells us what Sarah did when she hit the panic button. She had to do something to have a child, so she took things into her own hands. Sarah gave her maidservant, Hagar, to Abraham and told him to build a family through her. Sarah's plan worked. Hagar conceived and bore Abraham a son, Ishmael. Did it satisfy Sarah? No! It was only the beginning of new problems.

Isn't that what happens when we panic and take things into our own hands? We try to put an end to our waiting only to find we have created more problems. It is just when we feel most compelled to panic and act that we must try our hardest to wait.

Keep in mind: You don't crack an incubating egg. You must wait until the time is right for the developing chick to peck his way out of the shell. You don't prematurely slit a cocoon to release the butterfly. Last spring our son, Jason, found some caterpillars. The following day the caterpillars had spun cocoons on our carport. Jason watched the cocoons with excitement. Finally, he couldn't stand the wait any longer, and he tore open one of the cocoons. Out came a moth that could not survive. It soon died. The wait and struggles are necessary for proper development.

Christians, like chicks and butterflies, must go through periods of waiting and struggles. It is part of the growth process toward becoming a mature Christian. There are periods of waiting in our Christian development that cannot be rushed.

In this chapter we will explore how God renews our strength as we wait. God would never require us to wait without giving us the strength we need to sustain us during that wait.

Renewal

When we think of the word *renew,* we think of making something *like new again.* We talk of renewing magazine subscriptions and old friendships. The word renew has a different meaning in Isaiah 40:31. The Hebrew word for renew means to *change.* The verse could read this way, "Those who [wait] upon the Lord shall *change* their strength."

How do we change our strength? The key is in verse 29 of Isaiah 40. "He [God] gives strength to the weary and increases the power of the weak." Get the idea? We change *our* strength to *God's* strength. Renewing our strength comes from God, not self.

Isn't that what Philippians 4:13 teaches? "I can do all things through Christ which strengtheneth me" (KJV).

We must reach a point when we realize we are not all-sufficient. We cannot do it all, and we don't have all the answers. We must recognize our need for God and our dependence on Him. It is then that God can begin to renew our strength. We have to get self out of the way first.

I saw this renewal of strength beautifully demonstrated in my friend Cindy. She and her husband were in God's waiting room. They had tried for five years to have a child. They lost one baby. Later they decided to apply for adoption. Cindy admits going through various stages as they waited for a baby. She wrote these words shortly after they applied for adoption:

> In Matthew 26:39 Jesus taught us to pray, "Not as I will, but as You will."
>
> It takes some of us a long time to accept that. We want things our way. Sometimes we pray for something for so long, and it doesn't come. We wait and pray, and we have faith that God will answer this prayer.
>
> The weeks turn into months. And the months turn into years. We begin to ask, "Why won't God answer my prayer?" But we have been praying for something so specific we don't leave room for God to do what is best for us.
>
> Finally, we begin to realize God may have something different in mind for us. And we begin to pray, "Not my will, but Thine be done." Turning the decision over to God takes the burden off us. Our faith becomes strong again knowing God is going to do the absolute best thing

for us. It may not be what we had in mind, but God's wisdom is far greater than ours.

—taken from a letter written by Cindy Merritt,
Magnolia, Arkansas

Nine months after that letter was written, Cindy and her husband, Dennis, adopted a beautiful baby girl. Perhaps even more beautiful was the growth and the renewal of strength that took place in the lives of Cindy and Dennis as they waited on the Lord.

Not My Will, But Thine

Jesus prayed in the Garden of Gethsemane that the cup of death which He faced would be taken from Him. He prayed this prayer three times, and each time Jesus added, "Yet not as I will, but as you will." He had completely submitted to God's will, and we must do the same.

Accepting God's will for our lives is not always easy. We pray, "Thy will be done," but we sure hope God's will goes along with our will. We want things to turn out the way *we* want them to, don't we? One of the most important things in waiting is to stop looking for *our* answer and look for *God's* answer! How can God's will be accomplished if our own will is in the way?

God is not like an Aladdin's lamp. He will not spoil us by giving us everything we ask for just as a wise parent will not spoil a child. Rest assured, however, that God *does* hear our prayers, and He will answer them. His delays are not refusals. God never forsakes those who remain faithful to Him. He may ask us to wait, but He will never abandon us.

The following was cross-stitched by a friend and given to us:

Answers

Answers to prayers
Come in various ways,
Sometimes in minutes,
Sometimes in days,
And some take years
To fully unfold
The harvest of love
And blessings they hold.

Answers to prayers
Come in various forms,
Sometimes in sunlight,
Sometimes through storms.
Some blossom early
And some blossom late,
But each one will flower . . .
Have faith and wait.
—*Helen Inwood*

Harold Hazelip said, "God answers prayer by doing what *He knows* is best for us, not what *we think* might be good for us."[1] Can you recall a time when something you prayed for would have been foolish or maybe even disastrous? As time passes, we look back and realize God's will really was better than our own.

The first year I taught school I had a class of first-graders. All the college classes in the world cannot prepare you for the large amount of patience it takes to teach small children! I remember praying for patience as I taught those children. I have often laughed about how God answered my prayer for patience by sending me a new student, Zachary.

Zachary made the rest of the class look like ideal first-graders. The first day he was in my class, he kicked me, pulled off his shirt, and sat against a wall. I remember thinking, "But, God, I asked for patience, not Zachary!" Little did I realize that Zachary was God's answer to my prayer for patience. God was not going to grant me patience instantly. Instead God would give me situations that would help me develop patience. I learned to be careful about what I pray for because God may give it to me in an unexpected way.

Jesus said, ". . . your Father knows what you need before you ask him" (Matthew 6:8). God is able to renew our strength because He knows what we need. He may not answer our prayers with what we *want,* but He will give us what we *need.* The following poem illustrates this.

Answered Prayer

I asked God for power,
  that I might have authority over others.
I was made humble,
  that I might respect others.
I asked God for strength,
  that I might do great things.
I was made weak,
  that I might do better things.
I asked God for riches,
  that I might be happy.
I was given little,
  that I might be wise.
I asked God for greatness,
  that I might have the praise of men.
I was given meekness,
  that I might feel the need of God.
I asked God for all things,
  that I might enjoy life.

I was given life,
  that I might enjoy all things.
I got nothing I had asked for,
  but everything I had hoped for.
Of all humanity, I am richly blessed.

—*An anonymous soldier of the Confederacy*

Our idea of God's blessings includes material blessings, good health, happiness, and a life free from problems. God's idea of blessings may not fit this notion. His will for you and me may include suffering, illness, financial strain or heartbreak. God's blessing for the Christian is anything that draws us closer to Him. So, we can pray, "Thy will be done," knowing God will carry out those things that will draw us closer to Him. When we honestly say to God, "Not my will, but Thine be done," and we accept whatever God's will for our life is, we begin the renewal process. We change *our* strength to strength that comes from *God.*

Making God's Will My Will

How do we go about exchanging our will—our personal desires, wishes and goals—for God's will? It is one thing to say, "Thy will be done," but how do we live it? It must begin with the proper attitude. Our hearts must desire God's will in our lives above anything on this earth.

Sandra Woodroof Milholland described this type of attitude:

> It's a frightening proposition, but it seems to me that for the Christian, a time must come when he or she can pray, "God, I don't know what I really need; I don't know

what to do or where to turn, or what my talents are. But I'm yours and I'm ready to let you use me as you want to." To pray such a prayer takes faith, and faith takes courage. And the kind of courage that gives faith full rein is hard to come by sometimes.[2]

This is an attitude I have really had to work on. When Gary first began working on his doctorate degree, I would pray, "Please help this degree prepare him for a job at a Christian college." That was *my* will. I was praying specifically for what I thought would be best for us. Imagine my disappointment when Gary did not get the first job he interviewed for at a Christian college!

I finally realized how selfish my prayers had been and how small my faith in God's will was. My prayers have since changed to, "Lord, you know what is best

---

His delays are not refusals. God never forsakes those who remain faithful to Him. He may ask us to wait, but He will never abandon us.

---

for our lives. I trust you completely with our future. Lead us to the place where we can serve you best."

Once we have an attitude that is submissive to God's will, how do we recognize His will? Since God does not talk with us directly, how will we find His answers for our lives?

God's will is revealed to us in the Bible. You may say, "Yes, but the Bible doesn't tell me which job to take or when I will recover from this illness."

It is true that the Bible does not give us specific answers to every problem in life or tell us every decision to make. The Bible *does* give us principles to use in making our decisions. The Bible does tell us how to face our problems. God's will, as revealed in the Bible, gives us everything we need to know to make wise choices. It addresses all areas of our lives—marriage, raising children, work, temptation, the church. . . . The Bible tells us how to live.

If we are to know God's will for our lives, we must know His Word. That requires study and then application to our lives. How can we live according to God's will if we don't know what God's will is? There is no substitute for studying, knowing and loving God's Word. If you have not been reading the Bible, you may be amazed at its practicality. As you read you will see that God renews our strength through His Word. God's will can change our lives.

Below is a comparison of our will and God's will. Notice the scriptures listed under "Soaring with Him." As you study this comparison, you will see the contrast of a selfish life and a Christlike life.

MIRED IN THE MUD	**SOARING WITH HIM**
"My will be done."	"Thy will be done."
Is intent on self-glory.	Has true humility. 1 Pet. 5:5
Is concerned about other people's opinions of self; craves admiration and popularity.	Is increasingly free from the necessity for approval or praise of others. 1 Thes. 2:4
Is rigid, self-opinionated.	Is flexible. Ps. 75:5

Cannot stand criticism.	Handles criticism objectively; usually benefits from it. Prov. 23:9
Desires power over others; uses others for his own ends.	Is devoted to the common good. Matt. 23:11-12
Wants ease; is self-indulgent.	Ease given up when necessary; knows that many comforts precious to the self may have to go. Luke 9:23
Holds self-preservation of supreme importance.	Is aware that you lose your life to find it. Matt. 10:39
Tries to be self-sufficient; has a practical atheism by which he believes he does not need God's help.	Is acutely aware of his need of God in everyday life. Jer. 10:23
Feels that life owes him certain things.	Realizes that life owes him nothing; that goodness cannot earn him anything. Ecc. 12:13
Is oversensitive; feelings easily hurt; nourishes resentment.	Readily forgives others. Luke 6:37
Springs back slowly, painfully from disappointments.	Has capacity to rise above disappointments and use them creatively. Phil. 4:11
Trusts in material possessions for security.	Knows that security is in relationship to God, not things. Matt. 6:19-21, Luke 12:33-34
Indulges in self-pity when things go wrong.	Has objective resiliency when things go wrong. Rom. 8:28

Needs praise and publicity for his good deeds.	Works well with others; can take second place. Matt. 6:1
Is tolerant of, even blind to, his own sins; appalled at the evil in others.	Understands the potential evil in himself and lays it before God. Matt. 7:3-5
Is self-complacent; craves the peace of mind that relieves him of unwelcome responsibilities.	Knows that warfare between good and evil will not allow undisturbed peace. 1 Cor. 10:12; Acts 8:22
Loves those that love him.	Can love the unlovely; has a feeling of oneness in God toward all humanity. Matt. 5:46; Ps. 51:10

—*Marge Green*

Conclusion

"They that wait upon the Lord shall renew their strength . . ."(KJV). That renewal of strength is a promise! When panic sets in as we wait, we must change *our* strength to *God's* strength. We must draw our strength from His Word, the Bible, each day. We begin to gain confidence that God's will, not our will, is best for our lives. Only God can renew our strength.

[1]Hazelip, Harold. "Why Doesn't God Give Me What I Want?", *UpReach.* (Herald of Truth, Abilene, TX, Nov./Dec. 1984).

[2]Milholland, Sandra Woodroof. "Don't Lose Heart," *UpReach.* (Herald of Truth, Abilene, TX, July/August 1987.)

Sharing Session: Tell about a time when your will and God's will were not the same.

Action Guide: Pray specifically about what you are waiting for. Remember to include in your prayers, "Not my will, but Thine be done."

For Thought and Discussion

1. What does it mean to "wait upon the Lord"? How does this differ from ordinary waiting?
2. Discuss why some people panic when they wait. What are some ways people react when they panic?
3. What is the difference between drawing strength from God and relying on our personal strength?
4. We pray, "Not my will, but Thine be done." How do we distinguish between the two?
5. Tell of a time when God answered your prayer in an unexpected way.
6. Discuss how time is a factor in showing us that God's will is better. Recall a situation in your life when the passing of time proved God's will was better than your own.
7. How does God reveal His will for us? What should we do about situations in our lives that are not directly referred to in the Bible?
8. How do Christians wait differently from those who are not Christians?
9. Discuss the comparison of "Mired in the Mud" with "Soaring with Him." As a class, make a poster or bulletin board comparing the two.
10. What are some ways God has renewed your strength? How can you rely on His strength more?

4

Those Who Waited—Joseph and Job

I enjoy the study of Bible characters. It's so interesting to read about the lives of men and women in the Bible. As I read, I realize the times and customs are different from today, but human nature is the same. We face many of the same problems Bible characters faced, and we can learn a lot by studying their lives.

After I began this study about waiting on the Lord, I started thinking about various Bible characters who had to wait. The Bible is filled with examples of men and women who were required to wait upon the Lord. Hebrews 11 is referred to as the Faith Hall of Fame. It tells about great men and women who lived by faith. Do you know how that chapter ends? Verse 39 says, *"These were all commended for their faith, yet none of them received what had been promised."*

What's the point? These great heroes and heroines of faith died in God's waiting room. They were still waiting for what had been promised to each of them. They had learned what it meant to wait upon the Lord, and their faith did not waiver.

As I have studied the lives of these Bible characters, I have realized there are some great lessons that apply to all of us in our waiting experiences. We will look at some of these men and women to see what we can learn from them. In this chapter we will examine the lives of two men who waited on the Lord and had their strength renewed.

Joseph

Joseph has always been one of my favorite Bible characters, but I had never stopped to think about how much of his life was spent in waiting. Read Genesis 37-50 and notice all the situations in which Joseph was required to wait.

As a child, Joseph was a dreamer, and his family resented the implications of his dreams. Joseph waited over 20 years to see the dreams fulfilled. When he was 17 years old, Joseph's brothers stripped him of his robe and threw him down into a pit. Joseph waited in the pit, wondering if they would kill him or free him. Joseph's brothers sold him to a caravan of Ishmaelites, and Joseph had to wait to see what would happen to him and where he would go.

The Ishmaelites sold Joseph to Potiphar, one of Pharaoh's officials, in Egypt. The Lord caused Joseph to prosper while he worked for Potiphar, but the prosperity did not last. Potiphar's wife lied about Joseph, accusing him of making sexual advances to her, and he was thrown into prison. There he was placed in charge of the other prisoners. Genesis 39:23 tells us that the Lord was with Joseph and gave him success in whatever he did. Yet, he had to wait for his release.

While in prison Joseph interpreted dreams for Pharaoh's cupbearer and baker. Joseph was hopeful that the cupbearer would remember him after his release from prison, but Joseph again had to wait for two more years in prison before he was freed.

Joseph waited in Egypt for 13 years before he went to work for Pharaoh. He interpreted Pharaoh's dreams, and Pharaoh made Joseph the equivalent to our vice president. You would think Joseph's waiting was over, but it wasn't. Joseph waited seven years for the famine. During those seven years he was busy making preparations.

"Be assured that if God waits longer than you wish, it is only to make the blessing all the more precious."

Joseph's brothers came to Egypt to get grain during the famine. He waited to reveal himself. He sent them back to Canaan to get their youngest brother, Benjamin. How hard it must have been for Joseph to wait for their return! He must have looked for them daily, longing to see his brothers once again.

When they finally did return, Joseph once again waited to reveal himself. Genesis 45 tells the beautiful story of their reunion. Joseph knew it would be an emotional time. He waited until he was completely alone with his brothers before he said, "I am Joseph!" He told them to go back to Canaan and get their father, Jacob, and their families and move to Egypt. Once again Joseph waited for his brothers to return to Egypt with his father. Can you imagine the reunion?

Finally, Joseph waited to return to Canaan. Hebrews 11:22 says, "By faith Joseph, when his end was near, spoke about the exodus of the Israelites from

Egypt and gave instructions about his bones." Joseph was homesick. He knew Egypt was not the Promised Land. His last request was that his bones be carried back to Canaan when the Israelites returned (Genesis 50:24,25).

How did Joseph survive all those years of waiting? How was his strength renewed? What does his example teach us?

Lessons from Joseph

1. Joseph kept an attitude of submission to God. Read Genesis 45:5-8. When Joseph revealed himself to his brothers, he told them three times, "God sent me here." Later in Genesis 50:20 he said, "You intended to harm me, but God intended it for good to accomplish what is now being done, the saving of many lives."

These verses show Joseph's total submission to God's will rather than his own will. Joseph's will must have been to stay with his father rather than be thrown in a pit and sold as a slave. Joseph probably preferred to stay in charge of Potiphar's house rather than be in a prison. Yet, through it all, he believed that what happened was God's will, and God intended it for good. Joseph believed in the providence of God.

What about us? When things don't go our way do we pout and give up? Do we become angry and bitter? Or do we believe God must have something better in mind for us?

A Christian woman and her family moved to a new area. She was bitter about the move until a sister in Christ told her, "I know you did not want to move here, but I believe God brought you here for a reason. We need you here." The woman said her attitude changed at that moment. She realized God could use her anywhere, and He must have had a purpose in bringing her to that place.

2. Joseph continued to serve God. If our strength is to be renewed, we must be faithful to God no matter what the circumstances. There is a proverb that says, "Disappointments will make us better or bitter." Isn't that true? If we remain close to God and feed on His Word, even the worst of circumstances can help us become better people. On the other hand, if we turn away from God when things go wrong, we open the door for bitterness, resentment and anger.

God cannot renew our strength if we won't let Him. Like Joseph, we must be submissive to God's will and continue to serve Him even when we are waiting.

3. God seasoned Joseph. Joseph was in Egypt 13 years before he served Pharaoh. Why did he have to wait so long? God used those 13 years to prepare Joseph. The years spent in Potiphar's house and in prison helped Joseph learn the Egyptian customs, language and government. They also gave Joseph years to mature.

Perhaps God requires us to wait at times to prepare or season us. He knows we may lack the maturity or wisdom needed to handle the situation. God may require us to wait because He knows we are not ready.

An apple that is not ripe is not good. We tend to pucker at the very thought. God is like a farmer; He cannot gather His crop until it is ripe. God knows when we are spiritually ready to receive a blessing to our profit and His glory. God may cause us to wait to ripen us. Andrew Murray said in *The Believer's Secret of Waiting on God,* "Be assured that if God waits longer than you wish, it is only to make the blessing all the more precious."

4. Joseph knew how to forgive. Throughout the story of Joseph he never held a grudge. Imagine the difference at the reunion scene if he had! Instead of the expected revenge, Joseph forgave his brothers and showed them kindness.

Could we do the same? Often we have trouble forgiving little things. Or we may say we forgive someone, yet we continue to hold a grudge. Can God truly renew our strength if this is the case?

The story of Elizabeth and Frank Morris has been widely publicized throughout the United States. Their 18-year-old son, Ted, was killed in a car accident involving a drunk driver. While Mr. and Mrs. Morris were waiting for their grief to ease and the pain to heal, they found the ability to forgive their son's killer. Not only did they forgive him, but they taught him God's Word. Today the drunk driver who killed their son is a Christian. Mr. and Mrs. Morris found a renewal of strength in forgiveness.

5. Joseph always did his best. Joseph could have easily fallen into the trap of self-pity and said, "Poor, pitiful me. Look at all these bad things that keep happening to me. I give up."

Joseph's attitude was the opposite. He made the best of every situation. Genesis 39:2-5,21-23 tells us that even as a slave and a prisoner the Lord gave Joseph success. Notice it says, ". . . the Lord gave him success. . . ." Joseph kept going. He did the best he could do in fulfilling his responsibilities and then depended on the Lord to grant success. Renewal of strength comes from dependence on God, not self.

6. Joseph resisted temptation. Potiphar's wife repeatedly asked Joseph to go to bed with her. Joseph refused even to be near her. She was persistent, however, and one day grabbed his cloak and said, "Come to bed with me" (Genesis 39:6-12). Joseph left his cloak and ran out of the house. He didn't stand around to talk about it. He fled from the temptation.

People may be more vulnerable to sin while they are waiting. Satan knows this and will use any trick he can to get us to succumb to his temptations. Be on guard. God will give us the strength to say no. He has promised us He will never allow us to be tempted beyond what we can bear, and He will provide a way of escape (1 Corinthians 10:13). God renews our strength by helping us resist temptation.

Job

Job is another Bible character whose strength had to be renewed. Each of us can sympathize with Job when we read about the loss of his livestock, servants and children and later his illness (Job 1; 2). Each time I read about it, I wonder just how much one person can take.

Job knew what it meant to wait. He had to wait for the return of his health and prosperity. He waited seven days for his friends Eliphaz, Bildad and Zophar to speak (Job 2:13). Job had to wait for his grief to heal. He suffered a tremendous loss. Imagine the grief of suddenly losing seven sons and three daughters. Job 17:7 says, "My eyes have grown dim with grief."

Finally, Job waited for some answers from God. It is only natural to wonder why bad things happen. Job was no different. He spoke of his sorrow, his pain, and his lack of understanding, and he searched for answers from God. Job waited for a renewal of strength physically, emotionally and spiritually.

Could we endure the tribulations of Job? Would our faith in God survive such trials? What are some lessons we can learn from Job to help prepare us for such trials?

Lessons from Job

1. Job did not blame God for his tribulations. "In all this, Job did not sin by charging God with wrongdoing" (Job 1:22).

When problems arise people instinctively try to place the blame on someone other than themselves. A wise man said, "We need to spend more time solving our problems and less time placing the blame."

We must be careful about what we say is God's will. God gets blamed for a lot that is not His will. For example, if a loved one is killed in an accident, it may not have been God's will. It could have been the result of a bad choice, another person's carelessness, or of nature. Blaming God will only cut off the renewal process.

2. We may never understand all the "whys" in our lives. Our human nature questions why bad things happen to good people, but God may never show us why they happen. His wisdom and understanding is so much greater than our own. Notice what Job said in the following passages:

"How great is God—beyond our understanding" (Job 36:26).

"God's voice thunders in marvelous ways; he does great things beyond our understanding" (Job 37:5).

"You asked, 'Who is this that obscures my counsel without knowledge?' Surely I spoke of things I did not understand, things too wonderful for me to know" (Job 42:3).

Job's spiritual strength was renewed when he began to realize God's understanding is far above what we can comprehend. He may not have understood why such tragedy befell him, but Job kept trusting God, knowing that God knows what is best.

3. Job had confidence in God's eternal plan. He was able to look past the present with its pain and sorrow and focus on eternity. What hope! What renewal of strength! Job 19:25-27 expressed Job's confidence in a living Redeemer whom he would see with his own eyes after his death. He adds, "How my heart yearns within me!" Job looked forward to being with God in eternity.

Job thought of the tragedies in his life as tests to draw him closer to God. He says, "But He knows the way I take; when he has tested me, I will come forth as gold" (Job 23:10). He saw his problems as opportunities for growth and a part of God's plan. We, too, can find a renewal of strength as we set our minds on eternal things (Colossians 3:1).

4. Be careful how you encourage others. Job's wife looked at her husband sitting in ashes, scraping his boils with a broken piece of pottery, and said, "Curse God and die" (Job 2:9)!

Later Job's three friends came to sympathize and to comfort him. When they saw how great his suffering was, they sat and waited seven days before they spoke. When they did speak Job found no comfort in their words. In Job 16:1, Job called his friends "miserable comforters." Job's faith did not weaken in spite of his wife's pressure and his friends' words.

Our words can strengthen someone, or they can weaken someone. We must be careful about what we say to those who are grieving or hurting. Think before you speak. Ask yourself, "Will my words renew their strength or weaken it?" There are times when words may not even be necessary. Just your presence or a hug may strengthen someone. If you do not know what to say, just listen. Give the sufferer time to express his emotions.

5. Job went through a natural grief process. Healing does not take place immediately. Job waited on the Lord for his grief and pain to subside. It took time to work through his sorrow, but Job was patient. Happier days were in store for Job. "The Lord blessed the latter part of Job's life more than the first" (Job 42:12).

There are those we know who are waiting on a renewal of strength. They may be grieving over the death of a loved one, suffering from an illness, or hurting because of the pain of a broken relationship or divorce. We must patiently wait with them and allow them the necessary time for their wounds to heal. Give people the chance to work through their grief and pain. This will take some people longer than others.

One widow said, "My worst period of grief was not immediately following my husband's death but two years later. It was then I felt the real impact of his death."

We must be there for those who are hurting and waiting. We must allow them to express their feelings and work through their grief and pain in their own way. Pray for them, asking God to grant them a renewal of strength and happier days in the future.

Conclusion

What renewal of strength is in God's Word! The lives of Joseph and Job provide so many wonderful lessons for us. Oh, that we might keep their examples ever before us and apply the wisdom gained from a study of their lives as we wait upon the Lord.

Sharing Session: Look through the heroes and heroines of faith mentioned in Hebrews 11. Tell which of these Bible characters is a favorite of yours and why.

Action Guide: This week rejoice with someone whose strength has been renewed.

For Thought and Discussion

1. Prepare a journal that Joseph or Job might have kept. Share it with the class.
2. Divide the class into two groups. One group should act out the reunion scene between Joseph and his brothers (Genesis 45). The other group should act out how it might have been if Joseph had held a grudge.
3. Why do periods of waiting make some people more vulnerable to temptation and sin than others? How can we deal with the temptation without giving in to the sin?
4. Give examples of those who have faced adversity, yet continued to do their best.
5. How does forgiveness renew our strength? Find some Bible verses that teach us to forgive others.
6. What are some things people do today that make them "miserable comforters"? Contrast those words and ac-

tions with things that offer real comfort and encouragement.

7. Do some reading about grief, and report to the class the stages of grief. (Your local funeral home director may be able to provide information.)
8. Think of a time you have questioned why something bad has happened to you. Does God always reveal why? Read Job 36:26; 37:5; 42:3. Discuss how God's understanding is greater than our own.
9. What are other lessons we can learn from Joseph and Job that can help us as we wait?

5

Soaring on Wings

"... they shall soar on wings like eagles ..."

Throughout the Bible, objects from nature are used to help us understand God's love and care for man. Jesus spoke of the lilies of the field, the birds of the air, the farmer sowing the seed, and the pearl of great price. He knew His followers could identify with these objects and better understand His teachings.

Isaiah 40:31 also uses an object from nature to help us as we wait. Isaiah tells us that those who wait upon the Lord will soar on wings like eagles. That may not sound very exciting unless you know something about eagles. Hopefully, as you study this chapter you will understand what a wonderful promise this is. Even as we wait we can soar on wings and become "eagle Christians."

Many Christians never realize their potential to soar like an eagle. Phil Stapp, in an article titled "You Were Created to Soar!", tells the following story:

An Indian brave found an egg that had been laid by an eagle. Not being able to return the egg to its nest, he did the next best thing: he put it in the nest of a prairie chicken. The hen sat on the eagle's egg thinking it was one of her own. Eventually the eaglet was hatched alongside the prairie chickens. All his life, the eagle, thinking he was a prairie chicken, did what the prairie chickens did. He scratched in the dirt for seeds and insects to eat. He clucked and cackled. He flew in a brief thrashing of wings and flurry of feathers no more than a few feet off the ground.

Years passed and the eagle grew very old. One day, he saw a magnificent bird far above him in the cloudless sky. Hanging with graceful majesty on the powerful wind currents, it soared with scarcely a beat of its strong golden wings. "What a beautiful bird!" said the eagle to his neighbor. "What is it?" "That's an eagle, the chief of the birds," the neighbor clucked. "But don't give it a second thought. You could never be like him." So the eagle never gave it a second thought. He died thinking he was a prairie chicken.

The eagle never became what he was created to be because he listened to the world. What will you decide? Will you stay a prairie chicken, or become the magnificent soaring eagle God created you to be?[1]

Eagle Facts and Figures

Eagles have served as a symbol of strength and courage since ancient times. Five thousand years ago the Sumerians chose the "spread eagle" as their emblem of power. Centuries later Imperial Rome used the eagle as its emblem, and Napoleon I also adopted it. The ancient Assyrians used the double-headed eagle as their emblem. Later it reappeared on the imperial coat of arms of Russia and Austria. And the Congress of the United States chose the American bald eagle as the country's emblem in 1782.

About 90 miles from our home in West Tennessee is Reelfoot Lake. Each winter eagles migrate to Reelfoot Lake and stay there until spring. Hundreds of people go to Reelfoot Lake each year to observe the eagles. Many become so enthralled they return every year to watch these majestic birds.

What is it about this bird that represents such power? Why are we more fascinated by the eagle than any other bird?

Did you know that eagles . . .
—soar higher than any other bird?
—have an average life span of 30 years, and some have lived to be 100 years old?
—mate for life?
—are very protective of their nest and families?
—dwell on the rocks?
—have extraordinary speed?
—can carry objects equal to their own weight?
—have excellent eyesight?
—nest in concealed places to avoid conflict?
—have wing spans of six to eight feet?
—are 30 to 41 inches long?
—have the most vigorous wings of any bird?
—are the "king of birds"?

Perhaps that explains some of the reasons the eagle is so highly regarded. But how can that help us as we wait? What does it mean for us to soar on wings as eagles? Let us examine the secrets of why the eagle is so important to Christians

The Eagle in a Storm

When a storm approaches, most birds head for cover. Such is not the case with the eagle. The eagle can sense the coming of a storm long before it breaks. It will fly to a high spot and wait for the winds. When the storm hits, the eagle sets its wings so the wind will pick it up and lift it above the storm. While the storm rages below and other birds seek cover, the eagle soars above it.

Storms are a joy to the eagle, for they enable it to rise to new heights of glory. It soars effortlessly, letting the wind carry it where lesser birds cannot fly. The eagle does not escape the storm. It simply uses the storm to lift it higher.

Christians must face storms in our lives. Our storms may be sickness, tragedy, disappointment or failure. Our storms may force us into God's waiting room. We must choose whether to seek cover and hide throughout the storm like the lesser birds or be like the eagle and allow the storm to take us to greater heights.

The eagle anticipates the storm and prepares by flying to a high spot. Christians can also prepare for the storms of life. Matthew 7:24-27 contrasts a wise man and a foolish man. The wise man is the one who was prepared for the storm because his house was built on the rock. Christians are to be like the wise man and build our lives on Jesus, our rock. If our lives are daily centered on the foundation of Jesus and His love, we will be better prepared to handle the problems that come our way.

Eagles use the storm to lift them higher. Christians, too, can use the storms of life to take them to a higher level of spirituality. We can soar above the storm. That does not mean we won't be affected by the storm or that being in the storm will be easy. It is just that Christians can use the storm to grow spiritually.

All of us experience various storms of life. When the storms come, we can hide in self-pity and defeat, or we can rise above them by setting our mind and our belief on God. The storms don't have to overpower us. We can rise on wings of faith and allow the Lord to lift us up to greater heights.

Jane McWhorter is an inspiration to me. She is one who has allowed a storm to help her soar. Recently, Jane spoke to the ladies of our congregation. She talked about the car accident that almost took her life and the long recovery following the accident. She told how the accident helped her to more fully understand and appreciate God's grace and goodness. Her storm led her to greater heights of compassion for others, service and dedication to God's kingdom. Many lives have been touched and brought closer to God through Jane's example.

God never promised Christians that they would escape the storms of life. He did promise us He would help us to soar on wings like eagles. God can lift us up and allow us to grow to spiritual heights we could never imagine.

Paul wrote to the Ephesians to remind them of this. He said, "Now to him who is able to do immeasurably more than all we ask or imagine, according to his power that is at work within us, to him be glory in the church and in Christ Jesus throughout all generations, for ever and ever! Amen" (Ephesians 3:20,21).

Learning to Fly

The Song of Moses compares God's love and care for Jacob and the children of Israel to that of a mother eagle and her eaglets. Deuteronomy 32:10,11 says, ". . . He shielded him and cared for him; he guarded him as the apple of his eye, like an eagle that stirs up its nest and hovers over its young, that spreads its wings to catch them and carries them on its pinions."

That verse is an accurate account of how baby eagles learn to fly. John and Paul Sanford, in their book *Restoring the Christian Family,* describe the eaglets' flying lessons in the following way:

> An eagle mother trains her children to fly by an awesome process. A mother eagle flutters over her nest, demonstrating by sight how to fly. Then comes a day when she gathers an eaglet onto her back and spreading her wings flies high and suddenly swoops out from under! Down and down he plummets and perhaps begins to discover what his wings are for, until the mother swoops under him and catches him again on her back. Many times the process is repeated. If the eaglet is slow to learn or cowardly, she returns him to the nest, and tries again a few days later, and then perhaps again. But if he will not learn, she begins to tear her nest apart, until there is nothing left for the eaglet to cling to.[2]

Could it be God asks us to wait and allows us to experience trials because He is trying to teach us to fly? We try our wings, and we make mistakes. We feel as if we are falling rather than soaring, and there is God to catch us and bring us back to the safety of His fold, just as the mother eagle catches her baby.

God told Moses to tell the Israelites, "You yourselves have seen what I did to Egypt, and how I carried you on eagles' wings and brought you to myself" (Exodus 19:4). Isn't that a beautiful thought? It is such a comfort to know God will carry us on His wings and bring us back to His safe arms of love.

I do not know the author of the following poem, but it illustrates this point.

Under His Wings

As the eagle must force her young
  from the nest to teach them how to fly,
so our Father must press us out of
  routine to the things He'd have us try . . .

And just as the eagle guards her own
  to insure their safety in flight,
Our Lord is near when we try our wings,
  we're never out of His sight . . .

But should the eaglet begin to fall,
  the eagle swoops down from above
to rescue its young and bear it up
  on wings of strength and love . . .

So how can we doubt that the eagle's
  Creator, the One Who made us all,
would fail to save and deliver us
  if we should start to fall?

—*Author Unknown*

Do you feel yourself soaring on wings? Are you just learning to fly, or have you reached a point in your spiritual development where you feel God is helping you to soar like an eagle?

The Eagle's Renewal

David wrote, "He satisfies my desires with good things, so that my youth is renewed like the eagle's" (Psalm 103:5). This verse reveals another secret of the eagle's power—its renewal.

Eagles live and retain their vigor to a great age. Unlike other birds, eagles molt in their old age and renew their feathers. With the renewal of feathers comes a renewal of youth and energy.

No one seems to know exactly how the eagle molts. There are different legends and theories. One theory is that every seven years or so an eagle must renew itself. Its wing feathers become laden with oil and dirt and are cracked and worn from use. The beak and talons become calcified and brittle. It is then that the eagle retires to a cave or a place high beyond the reach of predators. There it begins the process of renewal.

Storms are a joy to the eagle, for they enable it to rise to new heights of glory. It soars effortlessly, letting the wind carry it where lesser birds cannot fly. The eagle does not escape the storm. It simply uses the storm to lift it higher.

This theory goes on to describe how the eagle uses its great beak to pull out its mighty feathers one by one. After the feathers are removed, it pulls out each talon claw by claw. Then the defenseless bird bashes its beak against the rocks until it too is broken, piece by piece. There the eagle waits until beak, talons and feathers have regrown. Through the process of waiting, the eagle's strength is renewed. If this theory is true, then even the eagle, the king of birds, must go through periods of waiting.

Perhaps our lives have become laden with the dirt and oil of sin, or we feel cracked and worn by discouragement and a lack of faith. God may ask us to wait as a part of a renewal process. He may be trying to draw our attention and affection to Him. It could be that when we feel defenseless, God is asking us to depend on Him rather than ourselves. When we rid ourselves of all the things that distract and burden us and place our complete trust in God, He begins to renew our strength

Conclusion

The eagle is a great symbol to many nations, but it is an even greater symbol to Christians. When God promised, "Those who wait upon the Lord shall renew their strength; they shall soar on wings like eagles," He promised us the ability to soar above the storms of life. He promised us strength and protection. The promise is there, but we must make the choice. We can choose to scratch in the dirt of life like the prairie chicken, or we can choose to soar like an eagle.

Let's be eagle Christians!

[1]Stapp, Phil. "You Were Created to Soar," Used by permission of *UpReach* (Herald of Truth, Abilene, TX, July/Aug. 1988).

[2]Sanford, John and Sanford, Paul. *Restoring the Christian Family* (Logos International, Kansas City, MO 1979).

Sharing Session: Give examples of people you know who have allowed the storms of life to lift them higher.

Action Guide: Write a note to someone who is an "eagle Christian" in your eyes. Thank that person for his or her influence on your life.

For Thought and Discussion

1. Read the following scriptures that refer to eagles, and discuss them in class: 2 Samuel 1:23; Job 9:25,26; 39:27-30; Jeremiah 4:13; Ezekiel 1:10; Proverbs 23:5; Revelation 4:7; 12:14.
2. Job 39:28 says that the eagle's stronghold is a rocky crag. How do Christians build their stronghold on the rock of Jesus?
3. Find additional facts about eagles, and share them with the class.
4. How can Christians prepare for the storms of life?
5. Find some Bible verses that describe God's protection for Christians.
6. Make a poster comparing "eagle Christians" with "prairie chicken Christians."
7. How can we help one another soar on wings like eagles?
8. The eagle is the "king of birds"; yet, it is an endangered species. Could Christians also be an endangered species? If so, how do we protect and add to the Christian species?
9. What are some other examples from nature that are referred to in the Bible that teach us great lessons?
10. Think of a time when God has seemingly carried you on His wings. Offer a prayer of thanksgiving for God's care.

6

While We Wait

"... they shall run, and not be weary; and they shall walk and not faint" (KJV).

I do not know anyone who *enjoys* waiting. Waiting can be very stressful. One of the hardest places for me to wait is in a doctor's office. The longer I sit and wait to see the doctor, the more I feel my level of anxiety rise. When I go to the doctor's office, I have to take a book or something to do with me to keep my mind off the wait, or I will go crazy. The waiting makes me weary.

What about the times we are in God's waiting room, waiting for our prayers to be answered or our needs to be met? How can we keep from being weary and fainthearted as we wait? How do we persevere? What are Christians to do while we wait?

The Weary and Fainthearted

The Jews to whom Isaiah spoke were waiting, and they knew what it meant to be weary. They had spent 70 years in Babylonian captivity. They had become homesick for Jerusalem, and they were discouraged. Now Isaiah was telling them they would return to Jerusalem. Although filled with hope and excitement, many of them must have questioned whether or not they had the physical endurance to make the 600-mile journey home on foot. Did they possess the physical strength to "walk and not faint" on their way home?

Today there are Christians who are weary and fainthearted. They have become discouraged as they wait, and they wonder if they have the spiritual strength to persevere. The faint include those joyless souls who find no gladness in God or happiness in His service. It also includes those who lack the courage to attempt anything and those souls who are open to temptation. How can they run and not be weary and walk and not faint?

Read Isaiah 40:28-31. In the King James version, each verse uses the words "weary" and "faint." First, Isaiah points to God who will not grow tired or weary. Next, he points to humans and says, "Even

When everything else seems to be going wrong, we can rest assured that things are right with God.

youths grow tired and weary, and young men stumble and fall" (verse 30). Finally, he brings these two opposites—the unwearied God and the fainting man—together in a grand thought: God is a giving God who bestows His power on the weary. When Isaiah writes, "They shall run, and not be weary; and they shall walk and not faint" (KJV), he is telling us that God will give us the power we need to persevere.

It is true Christians become discouraged and weary as we wait, but we do not give up. Someone said, "The waiters are the stayers in the race." We choose to keep running. We wait, knowing God will give us the strength to face each new day.

Waiting: how much is included in that word—faith, hope, endurance and strength!

Waiting Is Active

There are those who think waiting is a passive word. These are the people who do nothing as they wait. The word "wait" is a verb, an action word. I told an uncle of mine I was doing a study of waiting on the Lord, and he immediately quoted a little poem he had committed to memory.

> Be not weary in well-doing
> With a heart for any fate,
> Still achieving, still pursuing,
> Learn to labor and to wait.
> —*Author Unknown*

I like that poem because it gets across the idea that we must continue to be active even while we wait. We don't just sit back with our arms folded and wait. There is work to be done. Below are six things we can do as we wait.

1. Pray. There may be times in our waiting experiences when this is all we can do. We may feel so burdened and weary that we do not know what to say or exactly what to pray for. Even when we cannot form the words, God hears.

> But if we hope for what we do not yet have, we wait for it patiently. In the same way, the Spirit helps us in

our weakness. We do not know what we ought to pray, but the Spirit himself intercedes for us with groans that words cannot express. And he who searches our hearts knows the mind of the Spirit, because the Spirit intercedes for the saints in accordance with God's will *(Romans 8:25-27).*

Christians are so fortunate to have this avenue of prayer and to have the Holy Spirit to intercede for us. First Peter 5:7 says, "Cast all your anxiety on him because he cares for you." It is through prayer that we can give our burdens to God. A waiting Christian should be a praying Christian.

Some friends of ours had a 15-year-old son who suddenly became paralyzed from his waist down. They rushed him to the hospital. The doctors could not treat the paralysis until they could find what had caused it. They ran test after test and could find no reason for the paralysis. They told the family they would have to wait to see if the paralysis was going to spread or perhaps go away.

There was nothing anyone could do for this young man but pray. Word got out, and special prayers on his behalf were offered throughout this area in church services, at Christian schools, and in the homes of hundreds of Christians. James 5:16 says, "The prayer of a righteous man is powerful and effective." Within a week the paralysis went away, and our friends' son walked out of the hospital. His doctors still do not know what caused the paralysis or what made it go away. These friends will be the first to tell you there is strength and power in prayer when you are in God's waiting room. Praying is one thing we can do while we wait.

2. Listen to God. When we pray we are talking to God. We must also allow God to talk to us. There are times we may pray and pray, but we never slow down enough to let God speak to us. He talks to us through His Word, the Bible.

"Be still before the Lord and wait patiently for him" (Psalm 37:7). We live in a society that does not know much about how to be still. We stay in the fast lane, rushing from one place to another. We cram our lives with so many activities that we don't leave ourselves any time to be still. When we finally do slow down, we are usually so exhausted we just fall asleep.

The words "be still" (NIV) are translated as "rest" in the King James and New American Standard versions. They read, "Rest in the Lord . . ." How long has it been since you have rested in the Lord?

Jesus said, "Come to me, all you who are weary and burdened, and I will give you rest. Take my yoke upon you and learn from me, for I am gentle and humble in heart, and you will find rest for your souls" (Matthew 11:28,29). Jesus taught that as we learn from Him, our souls find rest.

Oh, how we need to be still before the Lord. We need to spend time alone with God reading His Word. We need to be still and meditate on what we read, rather than rush through it just to say we have had our Bible reading for the day. We need to think about how God's Word relates to our lives. We need to take the time to sort through our own thoughts and feelings and then concentrate on God's thoughts. It is here, in our time alone with God, we find encouragement, guidance and strength to persevere. Our souls find rest, and with the rest comes the ability to run and not be weary.

3. Obey God. The following two verses show that waiting on the Lord and obedience to God go hand in hand.

"Yes, Lord, walking in the way of your laws, we wait for you; your name and your renown are the desires of our hearts" *(Isaiah 26:8)*.

"Wait for the Lord and keep his way" *(Psalm 37:34a)*.

There are those who use their waiting as an excuse not to obey God. They question God's love for them and gradually grow away from God. They may not openly defile God, but they no longer demonstrate their love for Him or the Bible.

King Saul is an example of someone who did not obey God while waiting. First Samuel 13 tells the story of King Saul offering burnt offerings and peace offerings. Samuel had told Saul to wait at Gilgal for seven days and then Samuel would meet him there and offer the sacrifices. When Samuel did not arrive on time, Saul's men began to scatter, and Saul panicked. So, Saul offered the sacrifices himself rather than wait for Samuel.

Samuel realized what Saul had done and told him, "You acted foolishly. . . . You have not kept the command the Lord your God gave you; if you had, he would have established your kingdom over Israel for all time. But now your kingdom will not endure; the Lord has sought out a man after his own heart and appointed him leader of his people, because you have not kept the Lord's command" (1 Samuel 13:13,14). It must have broken God's heart to see King Saul disobey, and it breaks His heart when we disobey today.

Christians must keep obeying God's laws and keep doing what is right even when we are waiting. Obeying God can ease the burden of our wait because we can lean on Him for strength. When everything else seems to be going wrong, we can rest assured that things are right with God.

4. Look for good. "Be joyful always; pray continually; give thanks in all circumstances, for this is God's will for you in Christ Jesus" (1 Thessalonians 5:16-18).

There is good in every situation if only we will look for it. Too many times we find ourselves complaining instead of counting our blessings. Being thankful and joyful are attitudes every Christian must strive to cultivate. If we do not, our lives will be filled with self-pity. We will be miserable and make those around us miserable.

Paul told the Philippians, "Rejoice in the Lord always. I will say it again: Rejoice! . . . Do not be anxious about anything, but in everything, by prayer and petition, with thanksgiving, present your requests to God" (Philippians 4:4,6).

Our prayers should be filled with thanksgiving. Instead, we often rush into our many requests, and we never thank God for specific blessings in our lives. Our minds need to be trained to look for blessings and acknowledge them.

So much good has come from the waiting experience our family has had. I will confess, when Gary lost his job I could not rejoice, and I had a hard time being thankful. I did not want to return to Henderson at the time. Now, I can thank God for His providence. It has been such a blessing to be near my parents again and learn from their wisdom. Our boys have been blessed with the privilege of being close to their grandparents, and a special bond has formed between them. Gary and I are so thankful for the opportunity to be a part of the church in Henderson. Our boys have been blessed with some of the best Bible school teachers in the world. I am so thankful we were living here when my mother fell and broke her hip. Old friendships have been renewed, and new friendships have been established. The waiting has not always been easy, but we have been so blessed!

5. Do something for others. "Let us not become weary in doing good, for at the proper time we will reap a harvest if we do not give up. Therefore, as we have opportunity, let us do good to all people, especially to those who belong to the family of believers" (Galatians 6:9,10).

Dr. James Dobson says that some of the best therapy he gives to patients who are suffering from depression is to have them become involved in the lives of others. He says serving others takes their minds off their own problems, and this is often what the patient needs most.

There is a lady in our congregation who suffers terribly from arthritis. She lives with pain. Yet, I cannot think of anyone who takes food to more people, visits the sick and shut-ins more, runs errands for those who cannot, and has people into her home more often than this Christian woman. Her kindness and thoughtfulness have touched hundreds of lives.

Our lives may seem to be in a holding pattern as we wait upon the Lord. We may feel helpless in regard to our own circumstances, but we can reach out and help others. There will always be those who need a visit, a phone call, a letter of encouragement, food, financial assistance and spiritual guidance. You may be the friend someone has been praying for.

6. Prepare. "Therefore, prepare your minds for action; be self-controlled; set your hope fully on the grace to be given you when Jesus Christ is revealed" (1 Peter 1:13).

Any woman who has been pregnant knows what it means to prepare as you wait. For months we visit the doctor, fix up a nursery, and read books on birth, breast feeding and child care as we prepare for that special arrival of our baby. The preparation takes our minds off of our changing bodies and the anxieties that accompany pregnancy. Staying busy preparing for the baby makes the wait easier.

When Gary lost his job, he re-evaluated the goals for his life. He realized he was not adequately prepared to pursue the career he really wanted. He knew that to fulfill his goals, he must go back to school and earn an additional degree.

Patricia McMahan found out she had cancer when her son Kurt was only nine months old. When Kurt was three, Pat's cancer recurred, and the doctors told her it was terminal. Pat began to prepare for her death. She wrote, "My illness has given me the opportunity to decide how I want to weave the fabric of our days and nights together. I want few regrets and no compromises when it comes to influencing this precious human entrusted to my care."

Pat lived each day to its fullest. She wrote a journal for Kurt and painted pictures for his room. She prayed with him and taught him about heaven. She wrote the following in Kurt's journal:

> As much as we try to dig in our heels, this earth is not our real home. We are passing through on our way to eternity. And I know the greatest legacy I want to give you is a love of God and a strong desire to always put Him first in your life.

A few days before Pat's death, she told the minister of the congregation where she attended to tell the people their prayers for her had not been in vain. She added, "I am at peace with what is about to happen. When I die it will be victory, not defeat."

Pat had prepared for death. Her preparation inspired all those who knew her.

Are there preparations you could be making while you wait? How about your spiritual preparation? Have you prepared your mind for action so you can run and not grow weary and walk and not faint? Preparation is a part of waiting.

Conclusion

Psalm 37 is a chapter of the Bible I like to read when I become weary in waiting. It is filled with reminders for me to trust in the Lord, be committed to Him, give generously to others, and wait patiently. It is also filled with promises that God will be my stronghold in times of trouble. "Delight yourself in the Lord and he will give you the desires of your heart" (verse 4) and "though he stumble, he will not fall, for the Lord upholds him with his hand" (verse 24) are also precious promises.

This Psalm teaches us there is work to do while we wait. Waiting is not passive. If we will devote our lives to prayer, Bible study, obedience to God, service to others, thanksgiving and preparation for the future, we will find the necessary strength to "run and not be weary and walk and not faint."

Sharing Session: Read Psalm 37. Share a verse or a thought from this psalm that can help you while you wait.

Action Guide: Memorize Isaiah 26:8.

For Thought and Discussion

1. Discuss what it means to be weary and fainthearted.
2. Find Bible verses that assure Christians that God hears and answers our prayers.
3. Give examples of people who have had adversity, yet continued to do something for others.
4. How are we to be still before the Lord and rest in the Lord?
5. How can we make our personal Bible study more meaningful?
6. Have someone read to the class the words to the song "Be Still, My Soul" written by Katharina von Schlegel (*Great Songs of the Church,* Number 2, Great Songs Press, Abilene, TX, 1974).
7. Divide the class into five groups. Have each group choose one of the situations given below and discuss the following questions:
   1) How do we wait personally in a situation such as this?
   2) How would we help someone else who is waiting in this situation?
   3) How could we grow from an experience such as this?
   4) Are there biblical principles that apply in this situation?

Group A: Your husband is not a Christian. He attends services with you occasionally but has never shown a real interest in becoming a Christian. Seeing him obey the gospel is the desire of your heart. You are waiting. . . .

Group B: You and your husband want to have a baby, but you have not been able to conceive. You have been to different doctors for three years. You are waiting. . . .

Group C: You have a child who is now grown. You know he/she has quit attending church, and it breaks your heart. You are waiting . . . .

Group D: You have just learned you have cancer. You are facing several months of chemotherapy treatments. You must wait to see if the treatments will be effective and cure the cancer. You are waiting. . . .

Group E: Your husband lost his job due to a plant shut-down several months ago. He has searched for a job in his field of work, but thus far he has not been able to find a job. His unemployment checks will end soon, and your family cannot manage on your salary alone. You are waiting. . . .

7

Those Who Waited—Elijah and Jesus

The word *wait* used in Isaiah 40:31 comes from a Hebrew word that means "a rope stretched tautly." This Hebrew word is similar to the word *rope* or *cord* that is used in Joshua 2:15. That rope was the scarlet cord Rahab used to let down the two Israelite spies and save them from the king of Jericho.

The idea behind the Hebrew word for wait is that the waiting process can be a stretching one. It's not easy. It's a process that is often extremely difficult, but ultimately it has a good end.

I recall the tug-of-war battles I used to participate in as a kid at camp. Two cabins of campers would line up on opposite ends of a rope, and when the whistle blew, each team would pull with all its might trying to drag the cabin on the other end through the mud in the middle. I was on the victorious end a few times, and it was exciting. Most of the time, however, I was one of the ones who was dragged through the mud!

There are times in our waiting experiences when we may feel we are in a tug of war. We feel as if we are in the middle of the rope being pulled in opposite directions, dragged through the mud of life.

We may think we are being stretched to our limit, and we can sense that the Hebrew word for wait is an adequate translation. When we find ourselves in this spiritual or emotional tug of war, it is important to go back to the Bible and examine the lives of others who had to wait. "For everything that was written in the past was written to teach us, so that through endurance and the encouragement of the Scriptures we might have hope" (Romans 15:4).

Elijah

Elijah was a prophet of God sent to the wicked kings of Israel. Even though he had an apostate nation to reform, much of Elijah's time was spent waiting on the Lord.

We first read of Elijah in 1 Kings 17 where he told King Ahab there would be no rain or dew in Israel for the next few years. Following this, the Lord sent Elijah to the brook of Kerith. Ravens fed him bread and meat while Elijah waited for the drought to end. When the brook dried up, God sent Elijah to Zarephath to wait until it was time to tell Ahab that God would send rain. Elijah waited three years (1 Kings 18:1).

First Kings 18 tells the exciting story of Elijah and the prophets of Baal on Mount Carmel. Following the competition and the slaying of the prophets of Baal, Elijah went to the top of Mount Carmel to wait for the rain from God. He prayed seven times before he ever saw a cloud.

King Ahab told his wife, Jezebel, about everything Elijah had done. Jezebel sent a messenger to tell Elijah she would kill him by the next day. First Kings 19:3 says, "Elijah was afraid and ran for his life." If a wicked woman like Jezebel vowed to kill you, wouldn't you be afraid and run?

Elijah fled to the desert, sat down under a broom tree, and prayed that he might die. Then he lay under the tree and fell asleep. Here we see a man who knew what it meant to be weary and faint-hearted. Elijah had been stretched to his limit, and he was ready to give up and die. He was discouraged, lonely and physically exhausted.

God sent angels to minister to Elijah. They fed him, and he went back to sleep. The angels fed him again. The food strengthened Elijah, and he traveled 40 days and nights to Mount Horeb. There God told Elijah to go stand on the mountain. Elijah stood there

---

We may never understand the true reason why God asks us to wait, but we can be confident that God has a purpose and that His purpose for us will ultimately prove to be good. To God be the glory!

---

and waited for the Lord to pass by. There was a great wind, an earthquake and fire.

Elijah continued to wait until he heard a gentle whisper. God spoke to Elijah and assured him there were 7,000 in Israel who had not worshiped Baal. He sent Elijah to anoint Elisha to be his successor. God renewed Elijah physically, spiritually and emotionally. He gave Elijah the strength to "run and not be weary."

Later, in 2 Kings 2, we read of Elijah's final wait. He waited to be taken up to heaven. His companion, Elisha, was with him. They crossed the Jordan River, and Elijah turned to Elisha and asked, "What can I do for you before I am taken from you?" Elisha asked for a double portion of Elijah's spirit. Elisha wanted to be like Elijah.

We, too, should desire to be like Elijah as we wait upon the Lord. There are some tremendous lessons we can learn from him.

Lessons from Elijah

It refreshes my spirit to read about men like Elijah. We know Elijah was a great man of God because he is referred to many times in the New Testament. Some even thought Jesus was Elijah. Yet, even though Elijah was great, he became discouraged, lonely and tired. That helps me because I also become discouraged, lonely and tired. What can we learn from Elijah's example?

1. Elijah did not rush God. He waited for God to reveal His timetable. One would think Elijah was wasting time at the brook of Kerith, but he was there by divine command (1 Kings 17:1-6). Tony Coffey, a missionary to Ireland, wrote . . .

> Like Elijah, who was commanded to sit by the brook Kerith, we sometimes feel as if we are wasting time. By the brook Kerith I learned that spirituality is not always measured by activity. The busy life, the hectic schedule prove nothing conclusive. But the faith that honors and glorifies God sometimes must sit by Kerith.[1]

We must trust God's timetable. There will be times in our lives when God's will for us may be just to wait. We cannot rush God.

2. Elijah needed rest and food. When Elijah became so discouraged he wanted to die, the Lord met his physical needs first. He was exhausted. The angels who ministered to him said, "Get up and eat, for the journey is too much for you" (1 Kings 19:7).

There are times the journey may be too much for us as well. I heard a preacher say, "Sometimes the most spiritual thing you can do is get a good night's sleep." There is a lot of truth in that statement. I tend to make mountains out of molehills when I am tired. When I don't get enough sleep, I am hard to live with, and I become more susceptible to illnesses.

Our physical condition affects our emotional state. Jesus often met people's physical needs before He talked to them about their soul. If "the journey is too much for you," check your physical condition. Try to get adequate rest, proper nutrition and exercise.

3. Elijah needed to hear God speak. God spoke to Elijah in a gentle whisper on Mount Horeb (1 Kings 19:12). His words calmed and reassured Elijah and gave him the confidence to carry on.

In the last chapter we discussed our need to listen to God. God does not speak to us today with a still, small voice, but He does speak to us through His Word. Like Elijah, we need to be still before the Lord and hear Him speak. God can offer us the same reassurance and confidence He offered Elijah when we are discouraged if we will only listen.

4. Elijah needed a friend. He was lonely. Twice Elijah told God, "I am the only one left" (1 Kings 19:10,14). So God gave Elijah a friend, Elisha.

When we are waiting on the Lord, we need friends. We do not have angels to minister to us as Elijah did, but God has given us friends to meet special needs in our lives. Friends may meet our physical needs by supplying food or other things. More important, friends can help meet our spiritual and emotional needs by listening, encouraging, teaching and providing companionship. Burdens are half as heavy when shared with a friend.

5. Elijah eagerly awaited heaven. He expressed no fear or apprehension about leaving earth. We will not be taken to heaven in a whirlwind as Elijah was (2 Kings 2:11), but we can have confidence that we will live with God in heaven someday. Are we eagerly waiting for our home in heaven?

Jesus

One would think if anyone could have escaped waiting it would have been Jesus. If Jesus had never waited on God, how could He sympathize with us as we wait? "For we do not have a high priest who is unable to sympathize with our weaknesses, but we have one who has been tempted in every way, just as we are—yet was without sin" (Hebrews 4:15). Jesus understands what we go through when we are waiting.

Have you ever thought about why Jesus waited 30 years before He began His ministry? Luke 3:23 tells us Jesus was about 30 years old when He began His ministry. His ministry lasted about three years, less than one-tenth of His life span. Why was it so short? Couldn't He have reached more people had His ministry been longer?

The Bible does not tell us why Jesus waited until He was 30 to begin His ministry. We can only speculate. Common sense and experience tell us that wisdom comes with age. Jesus knew people would be more receptive to Him at the age of 30 than at the age of 20.

I have seen young men graduate from Christian colleges at the age of 21. They have earned degrees in Bible and are enthusiastic and eager to set the world on fire for God. Often their enthusiasm dwindles when they have a difficult time finding a full-time preaching job. They hear congregations say,"We want an older, more experienced man."

One young preacher told some elders who had interviewed him, "I can do something about my marital status and my education, but I cannot do anything about my age. I am sorry."

I think of those Bible majors with whom I graduated. Many of them became disillusioned for one reason or another and no longer preach the gospel. Were they perhaps too young to handle the problems ministers encounter or too young to earn the respect of older Christians? I don't know, but I can see wisdom in Jesus' waiting to begin His ministry.

Jesus used the first 30 years of His life preparing Himself for God's service. We know very little about those years. We do know He was obedient to His parents, and He spent time in the temple listening to the teachers and asking them questions (Luke 2:46,51). Those 30 years of preparation gave Him time to learn about human nature and how to deal with people. It gave Him time to know the customs of the land and the issues on the heart of the people. Chances are if Jesus had begun His ministry at 20, fewer people would have listened. God's timing is always best.

Another time Jesus waited is found in John 11. Lazarus became deathly ill, and his sisters, Mary and Martha, sent word to Jesus to come. They knew of

Jesus' miracles and were confident Jesus could heal their brother. Much to the surprise of His disciples, Jesus chose to stay where He was two more days. He waited to go back to Bethany. Why? Didn't Jesus love Mary, Martha and Lazarus? Didn't He feel compassion for them? Was He too busy?

Jesus told the disciples why He waited. "No, it is for God's glory so that God's Son may be glorified through it" (John 11:4). Jesus wanted to raise Lazarus from the dead, rather than just heal him, to bring glory to God. He wanted the friends of this family to believe He was God's Son.

At the gravesite Jesus said, "I knew that you always hear me, but I said this for the benefit of the people standing here, that they may believe that you sent me" (verse 42). Many put their faith in Jesus because of what they saw. God received the glory!

Lessons from Jesus

The Gospels are filled with lessons from Jesus. There are lessons we learn from His example and from His teachings. What does Jesus teach us about waiting on the Lord?

1. Jesus knew the importance of preparation. We noted earlier how Jesus used the first 30 years of His life preparing for His ministry. Much of His ministry was spent preparing for His return to the Father. Jesus had to prepare for the establishment of His church. He had to prepare His apostles for the work they would do after His ascension to heaven. He had to prepare for His death. These preparations were essentials.

In the previous chapter it was mentioned that waiting can be a time of preparation for us. We should prepare ourselves spiritually each day. We must prepare our children to carry on the work of the church. We must prepare to teach souls who are lost in sin.

Satan seeks to distract us from our preparation. He knows that if we are not prepared, we will be more susceptible to his temptations. Can we afford not to be prepared?

2. Prayer was a vital part of Jesus' preparation. It has been said over and over throughout this study that prayer is important when we are waiting. I do not believe we can stress prayer enough. Jesus certainly knew the importance of prayer.

Jesus prayed early in the morning before daylight to prepare for the day ahead (Mark 1:35). He spent an entire night in prayer before selecting His apostles (Luke 6:12). He left the crowds to go to the hills by Himself to pray (Mark 6:46). He prayed in private before Peter's confession that Jesus was the Christ (Luke 9:18). He prayed in the Garden of Gethsemane as He prepared for His death (Luke 22:41,42).

If Jesus, God's Son, felt such a need to pray, then don't we also need to pray? We need to be like Jesus' disciples who said, "Lord, teach us to pray" (Luke 11:1).

3. Jesus chose to wait in order to bring glory to God. Mary, Martha and the disciples could not understand why Jesus waited to come to Bethany. Thomas assumed it was because Jesus feared for His life. Actually, Jesus waited so more people would believe He was God's Son.

There are those of us who are like Mary and Martha. We wonder why God waits to bring an answer to our prayers. Larry Richards, in *When It Hurts Too Much to Wait,* says this:

This is something of the same mystery we face in our own times of agonizing waiting. Through the cross, we understand how deep God's affection is for you and me. We are sure that Jesus loves us as individuals. He is at home in our families and in our hearts. And yet there are times when pain comes and Jesus seems to stay away. . . . He lets us experience pain while He—and time itself—seems simply to wait.[2]

We may never understand the true reason why God asks us to wait, but we can be confident that God has a purpose and that His purpose for us will ultimately prove to be good. To God be the glory!

Conclusion

I am thankful I have a Savior who understands what it means to wait. I am grateful for the lives of Jesus and Elijah and for the lessons they teach me. I am thankful for the providence of God. I pray that the waiting experiences in my life can bring glory to His name.

[1]Coffey, Tony. "Elijah, Solomon, Apostles Instructed to Wait," used by permission of *The Christian Chronicle.* (Oklahoma Christian College, Oklahoma City, OK, Aug. 1987).

[2]Richards, Larry. *When It Hurts Too Much to Wait.* Waco, TX: Word Books, 1985.

Sharing Session: Ask each class member to share a lesson Jesus taught.

Action Guide: Be a friend to someone you know who is waiting on the Lord. Do something special for that person.

For Thought and Discussion

1. How is waiting like a rope stretched tautly? What are some of the stresses associated with waiting?
2. Discuss why our physical condition affects our emotional state. How can this also affect our spiritual well-being?
3. Read John 11:1-44 aloud in class. Ask various class members to read the conversational parts of Jesus, the disciples, Martha and Mary.
4. Find and discuss other times in Jesus' life when He had to wait.
5. Why are friends so important to us while we are waiting? Name some things friends can do to help.
6. Time your class in some activity (such as talking to each other) for one minute. Then ask the class to sit in silence for one minute. Which minute seemed to pass more quickly? Discuss the importance of productive activity while we wait.
7. Give examples of people who went through difficult circumstances that produced some good to the glory of God.
8. What are some preparations Christians should make? How can we make them?

8

Growing As We Wait

Have you ever known anyone who had "growing pains"? I heard about a teen-age boy who grew four inches in one year. His legs had stretch marks from growing so fast. I have known others who grew so fast their muscles and joints ached. Doctors diagnosed these aches as growing pains.

Just as our physical bodies may experience growing pains, our spiritual development may also produce growing pains. When we become Christians, we begin a never-ending growth process. We start as a baby (1 Peter 2:2; 1 Corinthians 3:1,2), and then we strive to grow into a mature Christian. But the spiritual growth process can be painful at times.

One of the painful aspects of spiritual growth is experiencing God's discipline. I am convinced that the waiting experiences of our lives are part of God's discipline and our spiritual development. As we wait upon the Lord and endure God's discipline, we undergo some spiritual growing pains.

Hebrews 12:1-13 discusses God's discipline. In this passage we are taught to endure our hardships as discipline. We must realize discipline does not mean punishment but training. Parents must discipline their children in order to train them how to live. God disciplines us to teach us. He allows us to experience times of waiting, struggling and pain to train us to be better servants for Him.

> Our fathers disciplined us for a little while as they thought best; but God disciplines us for our good, that we may share in his holiness.
>
> No discipline seems pleasant at the time, but painful. Later on, however, it produces a harvest of righteousness and peace for those who have been trained by it *(Hebrews 12:10,11).*

Waiting on the Lord can be very difficult, even painful, but these verses assure us that it is for our good. As we undergo the hardships of waiting, let us consider them as spiritual growing pains. We should ask ourselves, "How can I grow from this experience? What is God teaching me through this? How can this make me a better Christian?"

The last four years have been the most emotionally draining years of my life. The loss of Gary's job, moving in with my parents, the months of unemployment, the decision for Gary to go back to graduate school, the financial strain, and the uncertainty of the future have been hard for me. At times I have wondered, "Where is all of this leading us? Will we ever settle down?" But as I think back over the past four years, I can see growth. If waiting on the Lord has produced growth in our spiritual development, then the waiting has been worth it.

Joanne Howe tells the following story. It beautifully illustrates how pain and waiting are part of growth.

The Little Teacup

This is the story of an American couple who go to England. They are celebrating their 25th wedding anniversary. Both the man and his wife are fanciers of antiques, pottery and china. They come to a very famous shop called Susses, which deals in antiques, pottery and china. As they enter the shop, they single out a little teacup sitting alone on a top shelf.

"May I see that?" the man asks the shopkeeper. "I've never seen a teacup like that before. It's absolutely beautiful!"

Suddenly the teacup speaks. . . . "You don't understand . . . I haven't always been a teacup. There was a time that I was red, made of clay. My master took me and rolled me and patted me over and over and over. As he did so, I yelled out, 'Let me alone!' But he only smiled and said 'Not yet!'

"Then I was placed on a spinning wheel, and suddenly I was spun around and around and around. 'Stop it,' I said. 'I'm getting dizzy,' I screamed. The master only nodded and said, 'Not yet!'

"Then he put me in a hot oven . . . I had never felt such heat. I wondered why he wanted me to burn like that, and I yelled and knocked at the door. I could see him through the opening and I could read his lips as he shook his head and said, 'Not yet.'

"Finally the door did open . . . Whew! He put me up on a shelf and I began to cool. 'There, that's better,' I said. He only smiled.

"Then suddenly he brushed me and painted me all over. The fumes were horrible and I was gagging for air. 'Stop it, stop it, I can't stand it!' I cried. He only nodded and said, 'Not yet!'

"Then suddenly he put me back into another oven, unlike the first one, and twice as hot. I knew that I would not last and I began to suffocate. I begged, I pleaded, I screamed, I cried. And all the time I would see him through the opening, still nodding his head and saying, 'Not yet!'

"Then I knew that there was no hope and I was doomed to perish. I was ready to give up. But the door opened and he took me out and placed me on a shelf. One hour later he handed me a mirror and said 'Look at yourself!'

"And I did! I gasped, 'That's not me. It couldn't be!' I said 'I'm beautiful!'

" 'I want you to remember,' he then said, 'I know how it hurt to be rolled and patted, but if I left you, you would have dried up. I know how you must have been dizzy, spinning around on that wheel, but if I had stopped, you would have crumbled to pieces. I know it hurt and pained you while you were in that oven, but if I hadn't put you there, you would have cracked. I know the fumes were bad when I brushed you and painted you all over, but you see, if I hadn't done that, you would never have hardened. There would have been no color to your life. And if I hadn't put you back in the second oven, you wouldn't have survived for very long and the hardness would not have held. Now you're a beautiful, shining product for all to admire and appreciate. You're a finished product. You're what I had in mind when I first began working with you!' "

. . . Some of us are being rolled and patted and we can't stand it. Some of us are being spun around and we're dizzy from life and we object to it. Some of us are in the oven and it's all we can take. Others of us are being brushed and painted all over and the fumes are much too unbearable. Still others are in the oven twice as hot as the first oven and we still don't think that we can possibly survive.

And all the time we look to the Master and He shakes his head and says, "Not yet!"

The author and finisher of your faith is Jesus Christ. And when you become a new creation, the old life, the old pottery is thrown away and broken forever and tossed in the potter's field . . . for somehow that name has a comparison. But, the author of this new creation is Jesus Christ and He is also the finisher!

In 2 Timothy 2:20-22 it states: "In a great house there are not only vessels of gold and silver, but also of wood and earthenware; some for noble use, some for ignoble. If anyone purifies himself from what is ignoble, then he will be a vessel for noble use, consecrated and useful to the master of the house, ready for any good work."

Each of us who reads that story can probably think of times in our lives when we could identify with the little teacup. We sit in God's waiting room crying, "Let me out! I can't wait any longer!" and God answers, "Not yet!" God uses these times to consecrate us and purify us for His service. God allows us to experience spiritual growing pains to make us better servants for His kingdom.

Adelaide Pollard wrote the words to the hymn "Have Thine Own Way, Lord." The first verse says this:

> Have Thine own way, Lord,
> Have Thine own way!
> Thou art the Potter; I am the clay.
> Mold me and make me after thy will,
> While I am waiting, yielded and still.

We may sing the hymn, but do we really mean what we sing? Are we willing to be the clay in Jesus' hands? Are we yielding to His will as we wait upon the Lord? Are we willing to let God mold us into what He wants us to be rather than what we want?

God can help us to grow spiritually as we wait. It is His will that we grow. In the remainder of this chapter, we will examine five areas in which we can grow as we wait upon the Lord.

Growing in Faith

We grow in faith as we wait upon the Lord. Our waiting allows us to see just how weak and insufficient we are. We realize we cannot control all the circumstances of our lives. As a result, we learn to depend

---

God comforts us as we wait so we can comfort others. Who can sympathize with a widow better than another widow? Who knows the pain a divorcee feels better than another divorcee?

---

on God rather than ourselves. This is a hard lesson for some to learn. It was for me.

I am an organizer. I like things orderly and on schedule. When Gary lost his job, I realized I could not plan for things a year or two in advance, and it frightened me. I finally came to a point where I prayed, "God, I don't know what the future holds, and I am frightened by its uncertainty. Father, I know that You know what is best for us and You will work for our good. Help me to trust You more. . . ." At that point I began to put my faith in God's judgment rather than my own. It took a lot of pressure off me and helped me focus my dependence on God.

Isaiah 25:9 says, "In that day we will say, 'Surely this is our God; we trusted in him, and he saved us. This is the Lord, we trusted in him; let us rejoice and be glad in his salvation.'" Trusting God's will for our lives is an acknowledgment of our faith in Him.

Of course, we cannot grow in faith without growing in knowledge because faith comes by hearing the Word of God (Romans 10:17). Too many people try to make faith merely a feeling or an emotion. Certainly there are emotions involved in our faith, but faith must be based on knowledge.

Our confidence in God grows as we read His Word and learn of His promises. We learn to trust Him more as we read how He has proven Himself time and time again. We become more submissive to Him as we study His commands. It becomes easier to make decisions when our decisions are based on biblical principles. All of these blessings come from a knowledge of the Bible.

Peter wrote, "But grow in the grace and knowledge of our Lord and Savior Jesus Christ" (2 Peter 3:18). Growing in faith as we wait upon the Lord includes growing in knowledge. To grow we must study God's Word. Just going to worship services and Bible classes won't build a strong faith. We cannot expect to be spoon-fed Christians.

Spiritual growth includes growing in our love for God's Word and in our desire to study it. If your faith is not a growing faith, ask yourself, "Am I spending time with God on my own? Do I look forward to studying the Bible and talking with God in prayer?" If your answer is "no," begin today and make personal Bible study and prayer a habit.

Growing in Character

Waiting helps us to develop character. Character can be defined as moral strength. Paul told the Christians in Rome that their suffering would produce character. Growth would result from suffering.

> . . . we also rejoice in our sufferings, because we know that suffering produces perseverance; perseverance, character; and character, hope. And hope does not disappoint us, because God has poured out his love into our hearts by the Holy Spirit, whom he has given us *(Romans 5:3-5).*

Do you see the growth process in these verses? We can actually rejoice when we suffer because we know it will produce growth.

Job is a good example of this. Think of the suffering he endured; yet, Job emerged as a man of great character and faith. He never lost his moral strength. In the midst of his trials, Job said:

> But he knows the way that I take; *when he has tested me, I will come forth as gold.* My feet have closely followed his steps; I have kept to his way without turning aside. I have not departed from the commands of his lips; I have treasured the words of his mouth more than my daily bread (*Job 23:10-12* [italics mine]).

Job knew he was being tested, but his character was such that he said he would come forth as gold. God may use our times of waiting to test us. This can be a refining process to purify the character of our lives. Like the little teacup, the process may be painful, but it will be worth it in the end.

In 2 Peter 1:5-7 we are told to add faith, goodness, knowledge, self-control, perseverance, godliness, brotherly kindness and love to our Christian character. In essence, these qualities become our character. But God will not instantly give us these qualities. They must be developed. Our waiting experiences may be what we need to develop these qualities in our character.

Notice what happens when we develop the qualities of proven character listed above: "For if you possess these qualities in increasing measure, they will keep you from being ineffective and unproductive in your knowledge of our Lord Jesus Christ" (2 Peter 1:8). As we grow in character, God is able to use us more effectively in His service.

Growing in Compassion

Our waiting experiences help us to develop a greater compassion for others. We must keep in mind as we wait that God is aware of our struggles and that He is a compassionate God. He is called the "Father of compassion and the God of all comfort" (2 Corinthians 1:3).

Paul writes that God "comforts us in all our troubles, so that we can comfort those in any trouble with the comfort we ourselves have received from God. For just as the sufferings of Christ flow over into our lives, so also through Christ our comfort overflows" (2 Corinthians 1:4,5).

God comforts us as we wait so we can comfort others. Who can sympathize with a widow better than another widow? Who knows the pain a divorcee feels better than another divorcee? Who understands the feelings of a person with an illness better than someone who has experienced the same illness?

God may ask us to wait, to suffer, to struggle and to grow so He can use us to help others. Once we have been through something, God expects us to minister to others who experience what we have been through. God's comfort to others may actually flow through us.

We have a young woman in our congregation who has had two malignancies removed. She has undergone chemotherapy treatments and has been free from cancer for several years. Now she goes to other women who have had the same surgery and face chemotherapy. She knows how they feel, and she is able to answer their questions because she has been there. She can comfort these women in a way others cannot.

Lea Fowler of Newnan, Georgia, told of a time when one of her children was hospitalized, and they thought she was going to die. Mrs. Fowler was so distressed. She said her husband could not comfort her, nor could their preacher. She thought, "If only I could talk with someone who has been through this, I would feel better. They would understand what I am feeling." Her daughter lived, but Mrs. Fowler said she learned about the importance of compassion and ministering to others who are going through something you have experienced.

Gary and I lost our first baby. While I was recovering from the miscarriage, a friend of mine came to visit me. I still remember her saying, "God never allowed me to have children, so I don't know how to comfort you. After you make it through this, you will know how to comfort other women who lose a baby. You will be able to help them much better than I." That made a great impression on me. It helped me develop a greater sense of compassion for couples who lose babies. Now I have a responsibility to help them and comfort them in any way I can.

We grow in compassion for others when we have walked in their shoes. Our compassion leads us to service. Both compassion and service are necessary to achieve spiritual maturity.

Growing in Perspective

Waiting helps us grow in our perspective toward life and eternity. We lead such busy lives. In our efforts to achieve success and prosperity, we often lose sight of what is really important. The important things get lost amid the urgent things. Our waiting experiences can help us examine our lives, rethink our priorities, and focus on what is most important.

The loss of a job may cause one to rethink his or her career goals. It may also give a new perspective toward material things. The couple who is waiting for a child may focus on the importance of their marriage relationship. An illness or injury may cause one to appreciate one's health, family and friends. It can also give one more solitude to use for Bible study and prayer.

A cancer victim told of how her illness changed her perspective. She said, "I used to sit around and think about what my husband and I would do when we are 80. Now I don't look that far into the future. I try to concentrate on the present and live each day to its fullest."

Waiting helps us see another side of life. It may help us make changes that improve our relationship with God and others. It can help us get our priorities right.

Solomon was a man who had trouble with perspective. When he became king, he had his priorities in order. He asked God for a wise and understanding heart that he might rule his people well. God blessed him with those things and also gave him wealth and power.

The book of Ecclesiastes reveals Solomon's struggles with priorities later in his life. He sought happiness in wisdom, pleasure, prosperity and power, but he concluded, "Vanity, vanity. All is vanity." The word *vanity* means *meaningless.* All the power, wealth and pleasure were meaningless when put in perspective with eternity. Finally, at the end of Ecclesiastes, Solomon says, "Now all has been heard; here is the conclusion of the matter: Fear God and keep his commandments, for this is the whole duty of man" (Ecclesiastes 12:13).

Solomon teaches us to get our priorities in order. God must come first in our lives. Think through your perspective on life, the church and eternity. God may ask us to wait in order for us to gain a new perspective.

Growing in Patience and Perseverance

Have you seen the poster that says, "Give me patience, Lord, and give it to me NOW"? We can all identify with that thought at various stages of our waiting. Romans 12:12 tells us to be patient in our affliction and faithful in prayer. Yet, it is so hard to be patient when we are in the midst of a long waiting experience. We must learn to be patient with others, with God and with ourselves.

Patience and perseverance seem to go hand in hand. Perseverance is longsuffering. Some call it "stick-to-it-iveness." It means not giving up.

God does not give us instant patience and perseverance. We pray for patience, and God gives us the opportunities and experiences that help us develop patience and perseverance. James says it this way:

> Consider it pure joy, my brothers, whenever you face trials of many kinds, because you know that the testing of your faith develops perseverance. Perseverance must finish its work so that you may be mature and complete, not lacking anything *(James 1:2-4)*.

We all know how children can try our patience. I have often wondered why grandparents have so much more patience with children than parents do. Could it be that years of raising their own children helped them to develop the patience?

When I think of patience and perseverance, I think of a woman in our congregation who had to wait many years for her husband to become a Christian. She was so patient. She did not nag him to get him to obey, nor did she belittle him because he was not a Christian. There were times when she was discouraged, but she never gave up. She persevered in her faithfulness and in her godly life. Eventually, her husband became a Christian. This lady's example in patience and perseverance has encouraged others who are waiting for their spouse to become a Christian.

Perseverance and patience are vital to our spiritual growth. Just as muscles have to be exercised in order to grow, we must exercise patience and perseverance when we face trials if we are to grow spiritually. The muscles of patience and perseverance may be difficult to develop, but they have their rewards.

"You need to persevere so that when you have done the will of God, you will receive what he has promised" (Hebrews 10:36). Perseverance allows us to wait for God's timetable to unfold. We cannot rush

God. Any attempt to do so will only lead to frustration and disappointment. If we are patient and do not give up, God will reveal His plan for our lives. He may require us to wait a very long time, but God will ultimately work for our good.

Conclusion

There are those of you who are reading this book who know far more about waiting on the Lord than I do. Your waiting may have been terribly long and difficult. If that is the case, I am very sorry. However, if your waiting experience has brought you closer to God, then my sorrow for you turns to joy. If you have experienced growing pains that have produced in you greater faith, character, compassion, patience and perseverance, then it was worth the wait.

I challenge you to keep growing in the Lord. Share your perspective on life with others. Help them learn how to live each day to its fullest. Allow God to use you to His honor and glory. Praise God for renewing your strength during those times of waiting, and thank Him for His compassion and His providence.

Sharing Session: Share a lesson you have learned from your waiting experiences.

Action Guide: Memorize Hebrews 12:11.

For Thought and Discussion

1. Read Hebrews 12:1-13 aloud in class. Discuss how God disciplines His children. How does this help us grow spiritually?
2. Make a spiritual growth chart similar to a child's growth chart. Mark various signs and levels of spiritual growth on the chart.
3. What are other areas in which we can experience growth that are not mentioned in this chapter?
4. Sing the hymn "Have Thine Own Way, Lord." Examine the words of all of the verses and discuss their meaning.
5. What is faith? Read Hebrews 11 and discuss how these Bible characters grew in their faith. Who are some people who are living by faith today?
6. Discuss the Christian graces listed in 2 Peter 1:5-7. How do we develop these qualities? How do they enhance the character of our lives?
7. Name some opportunities God may give us to develop patience and perseverance. How is patience manifested in our lives?
8. How does God demonstrate His compassion for us? How did Jesus demonstrate compassion when He was on earth? What are some ways others have shown compassion to you? What are some areas you could demonstrate compassion because of your experiences?
9. Keep a journal or diary as you wait. Write down your emotions, things that helped you through the day, Bible verses that encourage you, etc. Periodically, look back through the journal. Do you see any signs of spiritual growth?

9

What Else Does the Bible Say about Waiting?

In the previous chapters we have studied Isaiah 40:31 in depth. I used to think that Isaiah 40:31 was the only verse that mentioned waiting on the Lord. I was so wrong! As I began this study on waiting, I discovered the Bible is filled with passages about waiting on the Lord, as well as examples of men and women who waited. It has been exciting to discover these scriptures and read words of strength and encouragement written to those who were waiting. We will devote this chapter to a study of those verses.

The format of this chapter will be somewhat different. The verses about waiting will be quoted without discussion. Following these verses there will be a summary of some of the lessons these scriptures teach us.

A variety of versions of the Bible have been used in the passages quoted below. I have tried to choose the clearest translation for each verse to help us understand its meaning. I would encourage you to read from other versions and compare them with the texts listed in this chapter.

I urge you to read each of these verses carefully. Take time to study it, meditate on it and pray about it. See how it relates to your life. Remember, it is God, not man, who is speaking to us in these scriptures.

Waiting and Hope

My soul, wait in silence for God only, for my hope is from Him. He only is my rock and my salvation, my stronghold: I shall not be shaken (*Psalm 62:5,6* NASB).

I wait for the Lord, my soul doth wait, and in his word do I hope. My soul waiteth for the Lord more than they that watch for the morning: I say, more than they that watch for the morning (*Psalm 130:5,6* KJV).

And now, Lord, for what do I wait? My hope is in Thee (*Psalm 39:7* NASB).

But as for me, I keep watch for the Lord, I wait in hope for God my Savior; my God will hear me (*Micah 7:7* NIV).

Waiting and Patience

If we hope for what we do not see, then we expectantly wait for it with patience (*Romans 8:25* McCord's Translation).

Rest in the Lord, and wait patiently for him (*Psalm 37:7* KJV).

I waited patiently for the Lord; he turned to me and heard my cry (*Psalm 40:1* NIV).

Strength and Courage as We Wait

Wait for the Lord; Be strong, and let your heart take courage; Yes, wait for the Lord (*Psalm 27:14* NASB).

O Lord, be gracious unto us; we have waited for thee: be thou their arm [strength] every morning, our salvation also in the time of trouble (*Isaiah 33:2* KJV).

Waiting and Obedience to God

Yes, Lord, walking in the way of your laws, we wait for you; your name and your renown are the desire of our hearts (*Isaiah 26:8* NIV).

Lead me in thy truth, and teach me: for thou art the God of my salvation; on thee do I wait all the day (*Psalm 25:5* KJV).

Wait on the Lord, and keep his way, and he shall exalt thee to inherit the land: when the wicked are cut off, thou shalt see it (*Psalm 37:34* KJV).

They quickly forgot His works; they did not wait for His counsel (*Psalm 106:13* NASB).

But you must return to your God; maintain love and justice, and wait for your God always (*Hosea* 12:6 NIV).

Happiness in Waiting

And therefore will the Lord wait, that he may be gracious unto you, and therefore he will be exalted, that he may have mercy upon you: for the Lord is a God of judgment: blessed are all they that wait for him (*Isaiah 30:18* KJV).

. . . Yet I will wait patiently for the day of calamity to come on the nation invading us. Though the fig tree does not bud and there are no grapes on the vines, though the olive crop fails and the fields produce no food, though there are no sheep in the pen and no cattle in the stalls, *yet I will rejoice in the Lord, I will be joyful in God my Savior.* The Sovereign Lord is my strength; he makes my feet like the feet of a deer, he enables me to go on the heights (*Habakkuk 3:16b-19* NIV [italics mine]).

Confidence in Waiting

I wait for you, O Lord; you will answer, O Lord my God (*Psalm 38:15* NIV).

We wait in hope for the Lord; he is our help and our shield. In him our hearts rejoice, for we trust in his holy name (*Psalm 33:20,21* NIV).

Indeed none of those who wait for Thee will be ashamed . . . (*Psalm 25:3* NASB).

Truly my soul waiteth upon God: from him cometh my salvation (*Psalm 62:1* KJV).

Do not say, "I will repay evil"; Wait for the Lord, and He will save you (*Proverbs 20:22* NASB).

I will wait for the Lord, who is hiding his face from the house of Jacob. I will put my trust in him (*Isaiah 8:17* NIV).

Since ancient times no one has heard, no ear has perceived, no eye has seen any God besides you, who acts on behalf of those who wait for him. You come to the help of those who gladly do right, who remember your ways (*Isaiah 64:4,5a* NIV).

The Lord is good unto them that wait for him, to the soul that seeketh him. It is good that a man should both hope and quietly wait for the salvation of the Lord (*Lamentations 3:25,26* KJV).

Waiting for Jesus' Return

And not only this, but also we ourselves, having the first fruits of the Spirit, even we ourselves groan within ourselves, waiting eagerly for our adoption as sons, the redemption of our body (*Romans 8:23* NASB).

But our citizenship is in heaven. And we eagerly await a Savior from there, the Lord Jesus Christ (*Philippians 3:20* NIV).

They themselves are reporting what kind of reception we had among you, and how you turned to God from idols to serve the true and living God, and to wait for his Son from heaven, whom he raised from the dead, even Jesus, who delivers us from the coming wrath (*1 Thessalonians 1:9,10* McCord's Translation).

While we wait for the blessed hope—the glorious appearing of our great God and Savior, Jesus Christ, who gave himself for us to redeem us from all wickedness and to purify for himself a people that are his very own, eager to do what is good (*Titus 2:13,14* NIV).

So Christ also, having been offered once to bear the sins of many, shall appear a second time for salvation without reference to sin, to those who eagerly await Him (*Hebrews 9:28* NASB).

Digging for Diamonds

The scriptures listed above are like diamonds for those who are waiting on the Lord. The longer we wait, the more polished and meaningful they become. As we incorporate them in our lives, their brilliance shines through to those about us. Let us examine some of the diamonds these verses teach us.

1. Wait on the Lord. Twenty-one of the scriptures listed used a phrase such as "wait for the Lord." The Bible does not just say, "Wait." It recognizes our total dependence on God rather than self, money or friends. By waiting on the Lord, we realize our helplessness and our weaknesses. We see our need for God. Waiting on God causes us to place our trust in Him.

2. Hope is vital. If you compare different versions of the Bible, you will notice the words "hope" and "wait" are used interchangeably. For instance, the New International Version translates Isaiah 40:31 as, "But those who hope in the Lord will renew their strength."

Christians wait with hope. The Christian's hope is not just wishful thinking. It is an assurance. "Now faith is *being sure of what we hope for* and certain of what we do not see" (*Hebrews 11:1* [italics mine]).

3. We must wait patiently. I am thankful God is patient with me. Aren't you? We must also be patient with God and acknowledge that His timetable is always best.

4. God strengthens us while we wait. We have noted this point in previous chapters, but these verses continue to reinforce this. God will give us the necessary strength and courage to wait—no matter how long it takes—because God is our strength.

5. We must obey God and love His Word. The verses above emphasize the importance of being teachable and moldable. Even as we wait we must maintain a close relationship with the Father through a study of the Bible and submission to His commands. Bible study and obedience should not seem like duties to the Christian but privileges.

6. We can be happy while we wait. Habakkuk had the attitude that, no matter what happened while he waited for God to invade the enemy nation, he would rejoice in the Lord. What a wonderful attitude! We need to be joyful like Habakkuk rather than filling our hearts with self-pity and depression.

Isaiah said that those who wait on God are blessed. The word *blessed* means the ultimate of happiness. We can be happy while we wait.

7. We can have confidence as we wait. Did you notice the expressions of confidence and trust in the verses listed above? The writers *knew* God would hear their cries and answer them. They were confident because God had proven His love for them; therefore, they could say, "I will put my trust in him." We can have that same confidence today. God *will* hear our prayers and answer our pleas.

8. Waiting for Jesus' return is the ultimate of Christian waiting. The Old Testament deals with the Jews waiting for Jesus, the Savior. The New Testament tells of Jesus' coming and His ascension back to heaven. Then the New Testament talks about Christians waiting for Christ's return. What hope should fill our hearts as we await our home in heaven!

We become so attached to things on this earth, and we often forget that all of this is just temporary. We lose sight of what we are really waiting for. New Testament Christians were *eagerly* waiting for Christ's return. We need to share that sense of eager expectation.

9. To God be the glory! God is exalted in our waiting (Isaiah 30:18). As God extends His grace and mercy toward us, He is to be praised. We should acknowledge Him as our shield, our help, our hope, our strength and our salvation. When God answers our prayers, we must give Him the glory. We have to get self out of the way and give God the credit and the praise. When others see God's will at work in our lives, they too can be drawn closer to God and bring glory to His name.

Conclusion

This chapter has been different in its design and content. The purpose has been to help each of us focus on what the Bible has to say about waiting.

The Bible addresses every need in our lives. For those who are waiting, God has spoken. He has instructed us, encouraged us, and given us the confidence we need as we wait for Him. The Bible is filled with diamonds waiting to be mined and polished by Christians. It should be a source of delight to us.

Let us say, as the psalmist David said, "Give me understanding, and I will keep your law and obey it with all my heart. . . . Oh, how I love your law! I meditate on it all day long" *(Psalm 119:34,97).*

Sharing Session: Choose one of the verses listed in this chapter that means a lot to you, and share it with the class.

Action Guide: Choose one of the verses listed in this chapter, and commit it to memory.

For Thought and Discussion

1. Have a devotional centered around the verses listed in this chapter. Assign the verses to several ladies who read well and ask them to read them in class. You may wish to include appropriate songs and prayers to make the devotional more meaningful.
2. Read the verses listed in this chapter from different versions.
3. Do a word study on the word "hope." Discuss how hope relates to waiting.
4. Read the verses in this chapter again. Underline key phrases that you feel are important to those who are waiting.
5. Read Psalm 119. Underline the verses that refer to God's law. Is it important for us to truly love the Bible? How do we show our love for God's Word?.
6. How do Christians demonstrate happiness even during difficult circumstances?
7. Are Christians today eagerly waiting for Jesus' return and their home in heaven? Why or why not?.
8. How do we give God glory? Find some psalms in which David gives God glory. Make a special effort to give God glory in your prayers.

10

Waiters, Beware!

Throughout our lives we receive warnings. These warnings are for our good and often protect us. Parents warn their children of possible dangers, and they teach them safety rules. Doctors may warn their patients of threats to their health and follow-up the warning by prescribing a special diet, exercise or medication. Railroad crossings provide a warning when a train is approaching. News bulletins and sirens warn us when we need to take cover because of a tornado or bad weather. Think of how many lives are saved because of these warnings.

The Bible also contains warnings, and many *souls* can be saved if these warnings are heeded. This chapter is a warning to those who are waiting. First Peter 5:8,9 issues the following warning:

> Be self-controlled and alert. Your enemy the devil prowls around like a roaring lion looking for someone to devour. Resist him, standing firm in the faith, because you know that your brothers throughout the world are undergoing the same kind of sufferings.

The Bible warns us that Satan, the devil, is out to get our souls. He prowls, seeking for ways to tempt us. Satan is good at disguising sin, and he may tempt us in very subtle ways. He has had a lot of practice, beginning with Eve. No one has escaped his temptation—not even Jesus.

After Jesus was baptized, the Spirit led Him into the wilderness to be tempted by the devil (Matthew 4). Following 40 days of Jesus' fasting, Satan began to tempt Him. Satan did not tempt Jesus immediately after Jesus came to the wilderness. Why? Satan knew Jesus would be more vulnerable to sin when He was weak from hunger.

Thanks be to God that Jesus was able to resist the devil's temptations. How did He do it? By standing firm in the faith as the above scripture states, Jesus was able to answer each temptation with, "It is written . . . ." Jesus experienced Satan's temptations; yet, he did not give in.

Hebrews 2:18 tells us, "Because he himself suffered when he was tempted, he is able to help those who are being tempted." What comfort and strength are in those words!

Satan knows us, and he knows the times in our lives when we are most vulnerable to sin. One of those vulnerable times is while we are waiting. If you are going through a waiting experience, beware! Satan is probably prowling around waiting for you to show signs of weakness. Be aware of your vulnerability, and be prepared to resist him by standing firm in the faith as Jesus did. "Submit yourselves, then, to God. Resist the devil, and he will flee from you" (James 4:7).

In this chapter we will discuss some of the sins that people who wait often fall prey to. Perhaps, by examining these sins, we can heed the warnings and become better prepared to resist Satan.

Bitterness

Not long after Gary lost his job, an elder's wife gave me some advice. She said, "Rosemary, don't allow this experience to make you bitter. It will only hurt you if you do." That is probably the best advice anyone gave me.

This elder's wife knew that during our times of waiting we are particularly vulnerable to bitterness. Waiting can prepare the soil of our heart for spiritual growth, but it can also provide fertile soil for the destructive weeds of bitterness. Hebrews 12:15 puts it this way, "See to it that no one misses the grace of God and that no bitter root grows up to cause trouble and defile many."

Beware! Satan wants you to become bitter. James 3:14,15 teaches us that bitter envy and selfish ambition are earthly, unspiritual and of the devil. That should be a clear warning to us to avoid becoming bitter.

Why is it so easy for that bitter root to grow in our hearts? When things go wrong in our lives, we often try to blame someone else. A football team loses an important game, and the players blame the coach for calling bad plays. A couple divorces, and each partner blames the other one for mistakes. Someone loses his job, and he blames his employer. Some people even blame God for the bad circumstances in their lives. As long as we blame others for the problems in our lives, we direct our anger toward them, and that bitter root begins to grow.

One of the problems of having the weed of bitterness in our lives is that other weeds usually grow along with it. "Get rid of all bitterness, rage and anger, brawling and slander, along with every form of malice" (Ephesians 4:31). Satan knows that when we become bitter, the door is open for other sins, too. Bitterness can deny us joy and rob us of blessings.

Larry Richards, in his book *When It Hurts Too Much to Wait,* says the following:

> This is one of the terrible things about bitterness—it so fills our hearts that there is no room for enjoyment of our blessings. Bitterness distorts our vision, and we just can't see the good things that are intended to remind us of God's care.
>
> . . . If you and I can only tear away the thick vines of bitterness that have overgrown the windows of our soul, we can look out and see the many blessings that God gives. And the vision of blessings can fill us with a comfort that concentration on tragedy denies.[1]

Hannah experienced this. All she could think about was her inability to have a child. Peninnah, Elkanah's other wife and Hannah's rival, continually provoked Hannah and reminded her of her infertile condition. Her husband reassured her of his love, but it was of little comfort to Hannah.

Hannah finally went to the tabernacle. "In bitterness of soul Hannah wept much and prayed to the Lord" (1 Samuel 1:10). Later Hannah told Eli the priest, "I have been praying here out of my great anguish and grief" (verse 16). Hannah hurt. She had waited so long for a child, and now the waiting was an emotional struggle as well as a physical problem.

There are many Hannahs in the world today. Although they may not have someone like Peninnah provoking them, each birth announcement, baby shower, and pregnancy of a friend is a painful reminder of their infertility. We must be sensitive to their struggle.

When Hannah prayed, she revealed her priorities. She promised the Lord that, if He would give her a son, she would give him back to God. Perhaps she was bargaining with God, but we know Hannah kept her promise. Her desire was for God to use her son in a special way. She was giving God, not self, first place in her life.

Larry Richards also wrote this:

> There's a vital lesson for us in Hannah's experience. When bitterness drives us to anguish and grief, it may be time for you and me to reexamine our priorities. The anguish and grief may be divinely engraved invitations to turn to God in prayer and to explore the motives that lie behind our fierce desires. It may be we need to know a change in motivation like that Hannah experienced. It may be that the area of our lives in which we remain so troubled needs to be abandoned more fully to him.[2]

The elder's wife who said, "Bitterness will only hurt you" was right. We must recognize the bitter root and deal with it before the weeds begin to grow. We should express our emotions rather than bottle them up. Confess bitterness and anger, and then get rid of them. We cannot find real joy and peace until we do.

Jealousy

Waiting often finds us looking longingly at the situations of others. When we do, we are vulnerable to the sin of jealousy and envy. Satan tempts us by saying, "Look what everyone else has. Just look at the people who are better off than you are—physically, spiritually and financially." Suddenly, we are not content with what God has given us, and jealousy enters our hearts.

Jealousy is an extremely strong emotion. It may start in our hearts as a small seed, but it eventually grows and will ultimately spill over into angry conflict. Jealousy is a quiet sin. There are no "big and little sins," but there are "loud and quiet sins." Jealousy may be hidden from others, but not from God. Jealousy and envy are listed among the lusts of the flesh in Galatians 5:19-21, right along with the sins of idolatry, adultery and drunkenness. Waiters, beware of the sin of jealousy!

Like bitterness, jealousy robs us of joy and inner peace. "A heart at peace gives life to the body, but envy rots the bones" (Proverbs 14:30).

King Saul is a good example of how jealousy can control our lives. First Samuel 18 tells of Saul's jealousy of David. David killed Goliath and then killed tens of thousands of the Philistines. When Saul real-

---

Satan knows us, and he knows the times in our lives when we are most vulnerable to sin. One of those vulnerable times is while we are waiting. If you are going through a waiting experience, beware!

---

ized David was more popular among the Israelites than he was, jealousy consumed him. Saul perceived David as an enemy, even though David was actually Saul's friend. Saul's jealousy, fear and anger led him to attempt to murder David. Saul could find no joy or inner peace. His jealousy led to other sins. If we are not careful, our jealousy can do the same.

It is so easy to become jealous when we are waiting. Those who are waiting for a job may be jealous of those who are doing well financially. The person who is waiting for grief to subside may become jealous of those who are able to laugh and carry on with life. Those who are lonely and waiting for a friend may be envious of those with many friends. A mother whose child has gone astray may find herself jealous of another mother whose children are faithful Christians. A childless couple may become jealous of those who have children. A working mother may be jealous of a mother who stays home with her children. On the other hand, a mother who stays home may be jealous of the success and financial security of the working mother. And on it goes.

Psalm 73 is a psalm of Asaph. Asaph makes a confession in verses two and three. He says, "But as for me, my foot had almost slipped; I had nearly lost my foothold. For I envied the arrogant when I saw the prosperity of the wicked." He says envy caused him to almost lose his spiritual footing.

Later in Psalm 73 Asaph explains a solution to his envy. Notice the following verses:

> When I tried to understand all this, it was oppressive to me till I entered the sanctuary of God; then I understood their final destiny. . . . And being with you [God], I desire nothing on earth. . . . God is the strength of my heart and my portion forever. . . . But as for me, it is good to be near God. I have made the Sovereign Lord my refuge; I will tell of all your deeds (verses 16,17,25,26,28).

Asaph's cure for jealousy was to turn back to God. He took his eyes off earthly things and put them back on spiritual matters. Asaph's key was to take God's view of time, to measure reality not by the present moment, but in view of eternity.

Solomon gave the same advice. "Do not let your heart envy sinners, but always be zealous for the fear of the Lord" (Proverbs 23:17). If we maintain a close relationship with God, we can keep the proper perspective and defeat jealousy. God wants us to be content. Satan wants us to be jealous. That is quite a contrast. Beware of the sin of jealousy!

Pride

A Christian mother feels as if her world is caving in. Her husband has quit going to church. She is having trouble with her teens at home. She is under tremendous pressure at work, and she is having a difficult time in her relationship with one of her co-workers. Her elderly parents are requiring more and more of her attention. Spiritually she feels dead, and she attends worship services merely out of a sense of duty. Tension and frustration are all around her. Yet, when others ask how she is doing, she replies, "Just fine." When someone at church mentions concern and offers to help, she responds, "I can handle it. I don't need any help."

Oh, the subtle sin of pride. It is pride that makes us feel self-sufficient. Pride keeps us from admitting we need God. Pride keeps us from asking for help or accepting help when it is offered. Pride focuses our attention only on ourselves. Waiters, heed the warning:

> Pride goes before destruction, a haughty spirit before a fall *(Proverbs 16:18).*

> When pride comes, then comes disgrace, but with humility comes wisdom *(Proverbs 11:2).*

I have a friend who was seriously ill. During her illness women from her congregation would come over and clean her house, cook, wash clothes, and care for her child. Following her recovery she said, "The hardest part of my illness was admitting that I needed their help. I have always helped other people, and my pride did not want me to accept help from them."

Satan has waged a campaign to convince us we can do it all and have it all. He rejoices when we depend on ourselves rather than turn to God for guidance and strength. But Satan is setting us up for a fall. We cannot do it all. We must recognize our need for God. Like bitterness and jealousy, the sin of pride will only hurt us and make our waiting more difficult.

Doubt

A teen-age girl is paralyzed in an accident and asks, "How could a loving God allow this to happen to me?"

A couple desires to do mission work. They are waiting because they have been unable to raise adequate financial support. They say, "Why is God making us wait when we are wanting to go share the Gospel in another land?"

A Christian woman becomes discouraged as she waits for her husband to become a Christian and asks, "Doesn't God hear my prayers on my husband's behalf? Where are the answers?"

Waiters, beware! Satan loves to plant seeds of doubt in our minds. His goal is to weaken our faith and pull us away from God. When we are waiting, we naturally question why. But if we dwell on the "whys," we become open to doubts. There are some things we may never understand.

Satan planted seeds of doubt in the apostle Thomas following Jesus' resurrection. He was distraught from the crucifixion and could not believe Jesus was alive again. Jesus appeared to Thomas and had him touch His hands where the nails had been and His side where the spear had pierced Him. Then Jesus said, "Stop doubting and believe" (John 20:27). Could He be saying the same thing to you and me today?

> But when he asks, he must believe and not doubt, because he who doubts is like a wave of the sea, blown and tossed by the wind. That man should not think he will receive anything from the Lord; he is a double-minded man, unstable in all he does *(James 1:6-8)*.

Do you see how serious doubting God is? It keeps our prayers from being answered. It draws us away from God rather than bringing us closer to Him. This is just what Satan wants.

Matthew 14 tells about Peter's walking on the water to meet Jesus. When he took his eyes off Jesus, Peter saw the wind, became afraid and began to sink. Jesus reached out His hand and caught him. Then Jesus said, "You of little faith, why did you doubt" (verse 31)?

There are those today who are drowning in the sea of life. The winds of tragedy, strife and conflict are causing people to take their eyes off Jesus, and they are sinking spiritually. Jesus continues to ask, "You of little faith, why are you doubting?"

We erase our doubts by increasing our faith. A life of little faith leaves room for doubt, while a life filled with faith is also filled with confidence and assurance that God works for our good. He knows what is best. There is no room for doubt.

Conclusion

"To be forewarned is to be forearmed," as the old saying states. The Bible has warned us of Satan's craftiness and his desire for our souls. We have been forewarned. It is up to each Christian to become forearmed, ready to resist the devil.

Ephesians 6:10-18 tells us to prepare for battle by putting on the armor of God. That armor includes the belt of truth, the breastplate of righteousness, feet fitted with the preparation of the gospel of peace, a shield of faith, the helmet of salvation, and a sword which is the Word of God. This armor equips us to resist the devil as we wait upon the Lord.

Waiters, beware! Heed the warning and be prepared.

[1]Richards, Larry. *When It Hurts Too Much to Wait.* Irving, TX: Word Books 1985.
[2]Ibid.

Sharing Session: Share your concepts of Satan.

Action Guide: Examine your life closely to see if any sin stands in the way of your relationship with God.

For Thought and Discussion

1. What are some other sins we tend to be vulnerable to when we are waiting?

2. How can we help those whose lives are filled with bitterness, jealousy, pride and doubt? How do we get these sins out of our own lives?
3. Ask a woman to speak to your class about the emotional stress that goes with infertility. Find out right and wrong ways to encourage couples who may be waiting for a child.
4. Read Psalm 73. Discuss Asaph's struggle with jealousy and how he overcame it.
5. What are the most terrible effects of bitterness? How does bitterness affect a person's relationship with others?
6. Who or what are you most likely to envy? When you sense jealousy springing up in your heart, how do you deal with it? Do you see jealousy as a problem in the church today? Why or why not?
7. Discuss the concept of "loud and quiet sins." Why are quiet sins so dangerous?
8. Think of times in your life when pride was a problem. How do we conquer pride?
9. How do we build a strong faith that will crowd out doubts?
10. Make a poster illustrating the armor of God. Discuss how it helps us resist sin.

11

Helping Those Who Wait

If you are not in God's waiting room at the present time, chances are you know others who are. You may desire to help them, but you don't know what to do. Too often when this is the case, we do nothing. We are afraid we will do or say the wrong thing, so we don't do or say anything.

Recently in our ladies' Bible class, we were discussing how to encourage those who experience trouble in their lives. One class member commented, "I think we do a really good job of meeting the needs of the sick and bereaved, but we fall short in helping those who experience disgrace in their family or those who are under emotional strain. We tend to act like the problem is not there." She made a good point.

The Bible is clear in teaching us we have a responsibility to help others:

> Carry each other's burdens, and in this way you fulfill the law of Christ *(Galatians 6:2)*.

> Therefore, as we have opportunity, let us do good to all people, especially to those who belong to the family of believers *(Galatians 6:10)*.

Therefore encourage one another and build each other up, just as in fact you are doing *(1 Thessalonians 5:11).*

We cannot ignore the problems of our Christian brothers and sisters. One of the beauties of the church is the help that is available through its members. Hebrews 10:24-25 teaches that one of the reasons Christians meet together is to encourage one another and to spur one another on to love and good deeds. We must become aware of the needs of those around us and then be willing to meet those needs if at all possible.

As mentioned earlier, many times we really do *want* to help, but we honestly do not know *how* to help. This chapter will focus on some specific suggestions of things we can do to help those who are waiting. Each waiting situation is different. You will have to examine the circumstances and decide which of the suggestions would be appropriate in that situation.

Pray for wisdom to know the right way to encourage someone, and then do it. Someone said, "It is better to do or say something, even if it turns out to be the wrong thing, than to do nothing. At least you cared enough to do something, and that means a lot." Whatever you do, do it in love.

Here Is How You Can Help

1. What should I say? Perhaps the hardest part of demonstrating our concern for others is knowing the appropriate thing to say. Proverbs 25:11 says, "A word aptly spoken is like apples of gold in settings of silver." What are some "apples of gold" we can say to those who are waiting?

A couple was experiencing marital problems. The wife was going to a marriage counselor. She was waiting to see if her marriage could be saved. She told me that she knew others were aware of their marital problems; yet, many acted as though nothing was the matter. She said the most appropriate comment others said to her was, "I am sorry you are having problems." She said that statement opened doors. If she wanted to talk about the problem she could, but if not she would say, "Thank you. I appreciate your concern."

To say, "I am sorry you are having problems" is not a prying, nosey statement. It does not make the other person feel defensive. It is simply an acknowledgment of your awareness of the problem and an expression of your concern.

Other "apples of gold" might include, "I am thinking of you"; "You are in my prayers"; "I hope this will be a good week for you"; "I wait with you"; and "Remember, I love you."

2. Pray. "The prayer of a righteous man is powerful and effective" (James 5:16b). Those who have been waiting a long time may become discouraged and feel as if their prayers are not being heard. It is such an encouragement to them to know others are praying on their behalf.

After Gary lost his job, I received a letter from a friend in another state. She wrote, "I want you to know that I am beginning tomorrow to pray for you and Gary *every* day. I've been doing it periodically, but I want to make an effort to do it daily." I saved that letter and still have it today because it meant so much to me to know someone was praying for us each day.

When you pray for those who are waiting, tell them. They may not feel the encouragement of your prayers if they are unaware you are praying for them. There may be times when you can pray together with the person who is waiting. This, too, can be encouraging and reassuring.

3. Encourage them spiritually. I have another letter I have saved. It is 11 pages long and was written to me at a time I was especially discouraged in our waiting. The purpose of my friend's letter was to remind me that God would not forsake us. In the letter she listed eight Bible characters who trusted God in their times of need. Then she wrote out Bible verses that would assure us of God's love, concern

---

When we show hospitality to those who are waiting, we are saying, "We will not desert you. We are your friends."

---

and power. She urged me to get down on my knees and pray. She even wrote out two prayers. What a friend!

I call the friend who wrote that letter "my Barnabas." The name Barnabas means son of encouragement (Acts 4:36). She encouraged me, not with flowery words, but with the Bible. She told me what I needed to hear.

"Therefore encourage each other with these words" (1 Thessalonians 4:18). We can truly help those who are waiting if we will point them to the Bible and reassure them of God's love. Encourage them to be faithful in worship—both publicly and privately. Share with them specific Bible verses that may apply to their situations. One friend said she read the Psalms over and over again while she was waiting, and now she encourages others to read the Psalms.

Remember to encourage in love and gentleness. A self-righteous, "I have all the answers" attitude is never appropriate.

4. Be a good listener. There are times when those who are waiting need to talk about their feelings. Anger, resentment and bitterness may have set in. These feelings need to be discussed rather than suppressed. When suffering or the agony of waiting spills over into words, we can listen.

Being a good listener means allowing another's tears to flow and their emotions to be released. We need to listen and try to be as understanding as possible. Be willing to listen without judging or advising, unless advice is requested. Sometimes talking about a problem and openly expressing the emotions that accompany it is the very therapy one needs. There are those who just need someone to listen.

5. Offer specific assistance. The type of assistance offered depends on the circumstances of the one who is waiting. We say, "Call me if there is anything I can do to help," but people rarely call. People don't know what we want to do or when we are free to help them. However, if we say, "I would like to baby-sit for you this Saturday" or "I'm bringing dinner to your family tonight," they are much more likely to accept the offer.

About two months after Gary lost his job, my "Barnabas friend" sent a letter with some money in it. The letter instructed us to use the money to go out to eat and see a movie. She said, "I know your finances are tight right now, and there is no money for recreation. Please use this money to go out by yourselves." She even suggested a good movie. The night out did Gary and me both a lot of good, but the expression of love and thoughtfulness did even more good.

When you want to offer someone assistance, ask yourself, "If I were in that situation, what would I like for someone to do for me?" Talk to someone who has been through a similar experience and get ideas of specific things you could do to help. Then follow through with the ideas.

6. Visit. People do not visit much any more. We have become so busy with our jobs, special activities and our children's activities that we feel we don't have time to visit others. As a result, there are a lot of lonely people.

One may receive a lot of visitors immediately following a death in the family or the onset of an illness; however, as the weeks turn into months, the visits may become few and far between. Think of those who could benefit from a short visit: newcomers, new Christians, widows, a new mother, homebounds, those facing a long illness or recovery, the lonely, those whose families are far away, those who are grieving, and visitors at church services.

Visits do not have to be long, and gifts need not accompany the visit. Just the gift of your time in making the visit can mean so much. It is a way of saying, "I care."

7. Send cards, notes and letters. There are times we cannot visit, but we can express our concern through a card or letter. If the waiting extends over a long period of time, send more than one card.

When my mother broke her hip, she received cards in the mail every day for over three weeks. One day while she was in the hospital she got 55 cards! She looked forward to the mail each day, and she read the cards over and over again. She especially enjoyed the cards with notes written in them.

When sending cards, don't just sign your name. Take the time to write a note, even if it is just to say, "You are in my thoughts and prayers."

Amy Hillyard Jensen wrote the following in the pamphlet *Is There Anything I Can Do to Help?:* "A sympathy card is a poor substitute for your own expression. If you take time to write of your love for and memories of the one who died, your letter might be read many times and cherished, possibly into the next generation."[1]

Written words of encouragement have one advantage over spoken words: They can be kept and read over and over again. They may brighten many days for those who are waiting.

There are those who say they just cannot express their thoughts in writing. There is a secret to writing: The more you do it, the easier it gets. If writing is especially difficult for you, buy an appropriate card and write, "This card expresses my thoughts." A passage of Scripture is always appropriate to write. You don't have to use flowery words to convey your concern.

8. Show hospitality. Romans 12:13 says, "Share with God's people who are in need. Practice hospitality." Hospitality can take on many forms. Basically, it is sharing what you have with others. That could mean sharing your home, your food, your time or your friendship. Those who are waiting may feel their circumstances have isolated them. They need the assurance that they have friends and that others care.

Patricia McMahan spoke to a ladies' Bible class one month before her death. She shared the following with her Christian sisters in that class: "When one's friends are confronted with major illness, it is very hard to know how to comfort them. It would be a lot easier to turn away and isolate that person. . . . I am very inspired to say that I have not had one friend desert me."

When we show hospitality to those who are waiting, we are saying, "We will not desert you. We are your friends."

9. Touch. A touch kindly given can show caring like no other form of communication. A touch can be a beautiful tool of encouragement. When we grasp the hand of someone who is sick, grieving, discouraged or fearful, it is one way of communicating that the person is not forgotten or forsaken. Touching affirms worth. We may not remember what someone says to us, but we will likely remember the hug, pat on the back, or touch of the hand. There are times this nonverbal communication may work better than anything we might say or do.

10. Share laughter. Those who are waiting may not find a lot to laugh about. If we can help people laugh, it could be some of the best therapy they receive. Laughter is God-given and sent to relieve stress, draw people together, lift spirits and lighten days.

Listen to what the wise man, Solomon said:

> A cheerful heart is good medicine, but a crushed spirit dries up the bones *(Proverbs 17:22)*.
>
> A happy heart makes the face cheerful, but heartache crushes the spirit *(Proverbs 15:13)*.
>
> All the days of the oppressed are wretched, but the cheerful heart has a continual feast *(Proverbs 15:15)*.
>
> A cheerful look brings joy to the heart, and good news gives health to the bones *(Proverbs 15:30)*.

A woman who was confined to her home said, "Share your humor. Bring *Reader's Digest* and read aloud. Describe what's funny out there. It may not tickle my ribs today, but tomorrow I may relish it!"

Your laughter is contagious. Share it with those who are waiting. It will make them feel better.

Conclusion

There are so many people waiting on the Lord who need our help. We must open our eyes and become aware of their needs. We need to become sensitive to their feelings and develop a greater sense of compassion.

"Each of you should look not only to your own interests, but also to the interests of others" *(Philippians 2:4).*

"Therefore, as God's chosen people, holy and dearly loved, clothe yourselves with compassion, kindness, humility, gentleness and patience. . . . And over all these virtues put on love, which binds them all together in perfect unity" *(Colossians 3:12,14).*

We must not sit back and do nothing. God uses us to do His work. First Corinthians 3:9 tells us we are God's fellow workers. We can help renew the strength of those who wait upon the Lord. A burden that is shared is not nearly so heavy. We can help others bear their burdens. In doing so, they can run and not grow weary and walk and not faint. Let us help those who wait upon the Lord!

[1]Jensen, Amy Hillyard. *Is There Anything I Can Do to Help?* (Pamphlet available from Medic Publishing Co., Redmond, WA, 1980).

Sharing Session: Tell how someone has encouraged you.

Action Guide: Send a note or card to someone who is waiting. Write out a scripture that you think would encourage that person.

For Thought and Discussion

1. Why are we better at helping the sick and bereaved than those with family problems or emotional stress? What can we do to improve?
2. What are some inappropriate things to say to those who are waiting? What are things people have said that have encouraged you?
3. Share some Bible verses in class that would be suitable to send to those who are waiting.
4. What are qualities of a good listener? How can allowing someone to talk about his or her feelings be therapeutic?
5. Divide the class into groups. Discuss some specific things we can do for the following: (1) the sick; (2) the bereaved; (3) those who have lost a job; (4) newcomers; (5) those with family problems; (6) homebounds; (7) those whose spouses are not Christians.
6. How can we help those who are waiting not feel isolated or deserted?
7. Make at least one visit this week. Who usually receives the most benefits from a visit?
8. Name various ways we can demonstrate hospitality.
9. Have class members tell some funny stories or have someone read excerpts from a funny book. Enjoy laughing together. Discuss the benefits of laughter.
10. Give examples of how Bible characters helped one another. (For example, how did Ruth help Naomi and Elisha help Elijah?)

12

Those Who Waited—Paul and the Prodigal Son's Father

When I find myself growing weary as I wait, I try to stop and examine the lives of Bible characters who had to wait. Suddenly, my waiting doesn't seem so bad.

I gain new perspective on life when I think of Noah's waiting and preparing for the flood and later waiting inside the ark for one year and 10 days. I think of how love motivated Jacob to wait for Rachel and work for her father for 14 years. I think of David who was anointed by Samuel to be king over Israel, but he had to wait for years before he actually ruled the nation. David also had to wait for his son to die as a result of David's sin with Bathsheba. Later, he wanted to build the temple for God, but again David had to wait and let his son Solomon build it.

There are many lessons for us in the lives of these men. When I read of their patience, their love for God, and their faithfulness to Him, I become aware of how small my own faith is. I gain strength from their examples that helps me as I wait.

In this chapter we will study two Bible characters who were required to wait. They are Paul and the father of the prodigal son. There are many in the world today who can identify with the waiting experiences of these two men. Unlike other characters we have studied, much of the waiting of these two men was spiritual in nature. Let's look at their lives more closely.

Paul

Saul was one of the last people you would have expected to become a Christian. Saul was an enemy to the early church. He held the coats of those who stoned Steven (Acts 7:58), and he tried to destroy the church by dragging men and women off to prison (Acts 8:3). He was making murderous threats against the disciples, and he asked the high priest if he could go to Damascus and take prisoners there (Acts 9:1,2).

While on the road to Damascus, Saul's life was changed. Acts 9, 22 and 26 all record the story. As Saul neared Damascus a bright light from heaven flashed around him and blinded him. Here Jesus confronted Saul by asking, "Saul, Saul, why do you persecute me?"

Jesus instructed Saul to go into Damascus and wait until he was told what he must do. The men who were with Saul led him by the hand into the city. For three days Saul was blind, and he did not eat or drink anything. He simply waited for someone to come and teach him. Imagine the things that must have gone through Saul's mind as he waited—the guilt, the questions, the prayers and the change of heart.

God sent Ananias to teach Saul. He restored Saul's sight and told him of God's purpose for Saul. When Ananias finished, he asked Saul, "And now what are you waiting for? Get up, be baptized and wash your sins away, calling on his name" (Acts 22:16).

We know Saul obeyed. God changed his name to Paul, and he immediately began preaching that Jesus is the Son of God. Later, Paul wrote this to Timothy:

> I thank Christ Jesus our Lord, who has given me strength, that he considered me faithful, appointing me to his service. Even though I was once a blasphemer and a persecutor and a violent man, I was shown mercy because I acted in ignorance and unbelief. The grace of our Lord was poured out on me abundantly, along with the faith and love that are in Christ Jesus *(1 Timothy 1:12-14)*.

But that was not the end of Paul's waiting. Paul told the Corinthian church that he was given a thorn in the flesh (2 Corinthians 12:7). We are not told what that thorn was, but most scholars believe it was some type of physical handicap. Paul waited for the thorn to be removed. Three times he pleaded with God to take it away, but God said, "No." Instead of removing the problem, God told Paul, "My grace is sufficient for you, for my power is made perfect in weakness" (2 Corinthians 12:9).

How did Paul react to God's answer? Did it weaken him? Notice Paul's response: "That is why, for Christ's sake, I *delight* in weaknesses, in insults, in hardships, in persecutions, in difficulties. *For when I am weak, then I am strong*" (2 Corinthians 12:10 [italics mine]).

Paul said it was his weaknesses, the things he waited for, that made him strong. How? Paul's strength came from God. His weaknesses caused him to depend on God rather than on himself.

Paul also had to wait for his release from prison. Paul went through many persecutions after his baptism. Some of these are described in 2 Corinthians 11:23-28. The list includes being flogged, beaten with rods, stoned, imprisoned and other persecutions.

Paul certainly didn't exchange his life as a persecutor of the church for an easier life.

While in prison in Rome, Paul wrote a letter to the Christians in Philippi. In his letter he wrote about waiting to be delivered from prison. He also wrote about waiting for a greater deliverance when he would die and go to be with Jesus. Paul wrote, "For to me, to live is Christ and to die is gain. . . . I am torn between the two: I desire to depart and be with Christ, which is better by far; but it is more necessary for you that I remain in the body" (Philippians 1:21,23,24).

Paul knew about waiting. He waited for someone to teach him the truth, for his thorn to be removed, for release from prison, and for death so that he could be with Christ.

Lessons from Paul

1. There are people who are waiting for us to teach them the truth. Saul waited for Ananias to teach him. Ananias was hesitant. He told the Lord all the bad things he had heard about Saul. Ananias was afraid, but the Lord said, "Go!"

Aren't we like Ananias at times? We see those around us who are living in sin. We know they are lost, but we are hesitant to go teach them. Why? We are afraid they won't listen or they will reject the truth. We are afraid they won't be our friends anymore. We are afraid we might offend them. But God says, "Go, anyway!"

What if Ananias had never gone to Saul? Saul might have been lost. What if we don't go to those who are waiting to hear the gospel? We cannot afford to hesitate or let our fears keep us from teaching others.

Matthew 13 tells the parable of the sower. We are like the farmer in the parable. We are to sow the seed by teaching God's Word. We sow the seed and then wait for the seed to grow. It will fall on different types of soil. Some will obey, and some will not. We are not to judge the soil of people's hearts. We are just to plant the seed.

> So neither he who plants nor he who waters is anything, but only God, who makes things grow. The man who plants and the man who waters have one purpose, and each one will be rewarded according to his own labor *(1 Corinthians 3:7,8)*.

Look around you. Is there someone waiting for you to teach him? Let's open our eyes to the opportunities to teach God's Word.

2. "What are you waiting for?" Ananias asked Saul this question. The same question applies to those today who have heard the truth, yet have never obeyed it. What are you waiting for? Why are you not a Christian? Why won't you obey?

If you are a Christian, but your commitment to Christ is not what it should be, what are you waiting for? When will you come back to Jesus and allow Him to be the Lord of your life? Don't wait. Satan may harden your heart if you wait too long. Seriously consider the question Ananias asked Saul, "What are you waiting for?"

3. God may say "no" to some of our requests. God did not remove Paul's thorn in the flesh even though Paul pleaded with Him to do so. God was not punishing Paul. He was making Paul stronger.

We must continually remind ourselves that God knows what is best for us. If God says no to our prayer, it's for our own good. God may allow us to become weak in order to make us stronger in our faith and dependence on him.

We may not understand why God says no, but with each no comes the reminder, "My grace is sufficient for you, for my power is made perfect in weakness" (2 Corinthians 12:9).

4. Our waiting has a purpose. Paul's imprisonment in Rome seems like a terrible thing; yet, while in prison Paul wrote, ". . . what has happened to me has really served to advance the gospel" (Philippians 1:12). God used Paul's waiting situation to help others learn about the Gospel. God can take the circumstances we think are bad and use them for good.

Some close friends of ours have a small child who is waiting for a liver transplant. When I talked with the mother of this child after a previous operation, she described the many opportunities she and her husband have had to talk with other parents and nurses at the hospital about Christ. She said, "I can't imagine going through this without Christ."

Not all circumstances are good, but God can use these circumstances to advance the Gospel. He has a purpose in our waiting.

5. To be with Christ is better by far. This is what Paul said as he contemplated death. He was eager to live with Christ. Paul also wrote, "For our light and momentary troubles are achieving for us an eternal glory that far outweighs them all" (2 Corinthians 4:17).

Most people fear death. We enjoy living, and we don't want to die. As we face the death of a loved one or our own death, we need the constant reassurance that to be with Christ is better by far. "Precious in the sight of the Lord is the death of his saints" (Psalm 116:15). Christians don't need to fear death. We are going on to something better.

The Prodigal Son's Father

One of the most touching stories in the Bible is the parable of the prodigal son. The word *prodigal* means *exceedingly wasteful.* It is a good description of the younger son who asked his father for his inheritance. The son took the money, went to a distant country, and wasted his wealth in wild living. He wound up feeding pigs.

It must have been hard for this boy's father to see his son leave. The father was aware of the impetuousness of youth, and he must have known his son would make mistakes. While the son was away, there must have been an emptiness inside the father, a longing to know of his son's safety and welfare. Many prayers were probably offered on his son's behalf.

We don't know how long the son was away. We do know the father continually looked for his son. Luke 15:20 says, "But while he was still a long way off, his father saw him and was filled with compassion for him; he ran to his son, threw his arms around him and kissed him."

What a homecoming! Can you imagine the tears that were shed and the great celebration that followed? This father had waited for his youngest son to return, and now he was home. The father's waiting was over.

Lessons from the Father

1. God waits for His children who stray. The father in this parable represents God, our heavenly Father. In the church there are prodigal Christians, those who are wasting their talent, wealth and time by seeking pleasure, power and possessions. They have left their spiritual Father. Even though they have gone astray, God continues to love them, and He is waiting for them to return.

Throughout this book we have discussed how we wait upon the Lord. Have you ever thought about how God also waits? He longs for those who have left Him to return.

When the prodigal son returned, his father accepted him back without asking questions or waiting until he could prove himself to be a good son. God does the same for His children. If we repent and ask for God's forgiveness, God forgives us immediately. He doesn't remember the bad things we have done. Unlike humans, when God forgives, He forgets.

"How great is the love the Father has lavished on us, that we should be called children of God! And

Not all circumstances are good, but God can use these circumstances to advance the gospel. He has a purpose in our waiting.

that is what we are" (1 John 3:1)! What a loving, heavenly Father!

2. We should never quit waiting for those who have left their spiritual Father to return. The lost son's father did not give up. He kept waiting and hoping.

There are parents who can identify with the father because their sons or daughters have stopped going to church and have lost interest in spiritual things. Don't give up! There are others waiting for spouses, brothers, sisters or friends to come back to God. Keep waiting! God is waiting with you. He, too, is anxious for their return.

There was a Christian mother who had waited for years to see her children come back to church. She never quit praying for them. Her final request was that her funeral be held at the church building where she had attended. Her funeral brought her children inside the church building for the first time in years. Shortly after her death, the children came back to the Father and were restored. Her waiting and her prayers paid off.

3. Wait with compassion. When the father saw his lost son, he was filled with compassion for him. He got a robe, a ring, sandals and food for the boy. His compassion was demonstrated by his love and acceptance.

Christians are commanded to be compassionate people. "Be kind and compassionate to one another, forgiving each other, just as in Christ God forgave you" (Ephesians 4:32).

Compassion is an emotion. It is being able to sympathize with another and feel some of what the other is going through. Compassion usually goes hand in hand with kindness. Our feelings prompt us to take action that will help ease another's burdens. Think of how many straying Christians might return to God if they were treated with compassion rather than impatience, bitterness or harsh judgment.

4. When our waiting is over, it is time for a celebration. The father was so happy to have his son home. He said, "Bring the fattened calf and kill it. Let's have a feast and celebrate" (Luke 15:23). He certainly had a good reason to celebrate.

Luke 15 also records the parables of the lost sheep and the lost coin. In both parables there was a celebration and great rejoicing when the lost items were found. Romans 12:15 tells us to rejoice with those who rejoice and weep with those who weep. Sometimes we do a better job of weeping with others than we do rejoicing with those who have a reason to celebrate.

Our celebrations do not have to be parties. Worship can be a celebration. When our waiting has ended, our prayers should be a celebration of thanksgiving. The Psalms are good examples of this. We should thank God for hearing and answering our prayers, for strengthening and sustaining us, for providing us with Christian friends who helped us, and for His power which has worked great things.

Our celebrations should be a time to give God the glory. Paul told Timothy, "Now to the King eternal, immortal, invisible, the only God, be honor and glory for ever and ever. Amen" (1 Timothy 1:17).

When some friends of ours adopted a baby, the adoption agency had a celebration ceremony. They gave the couple the baby. Then the social worker and those associated with the adoption agency each said something to the new parents. Scriptures were read, and prayers were offered. The ceremony was videotaped and presented to the adoptive parents. Our friends say this celebration will be one of their most precious moments.

Luke 15 teaches us there is rejoicing in heaven

when one sinner repents. If God and the angels can celebrate, shouldn't we?

Conclusion

Paul and the father of the prodigal son are good examples for those who are waiting for a loved one to obey the gospel or return to the church. They teach us of God's loving, compassionate nature. They instruct us to keep the priorities in our lives focused on spiritual matters rather than earthly things. They challenge us to teach and serve others. Most important, they remind us of heaven. There will be no waiting in heaven. It will be better by far than anything we have known on earth. And there is no doubt—it is worth waiting for!

Sharing Session: Tell about the person(s) who taught you the gospel.

Action Guide: Think of some people you love who are not Christians. Use any opportunity you may have to teach them about Jesus. Pray for Christians who have strayed away from the church.

For Thought and Discussion

1. Discuss how the following Bible characters had to wait upon the Lord: Noah, Jacob and David. What are some lessons we can learn from them?
2. Do a character study of Moses. List the things for which he waited. Discuss some lessons we can learn from Moses that can help us as we wait.

3. Give examples of times when God answered your prayer with "no." How has this worked for your good?
4. Why do people fear death? How can we prepare for death? Ask a class member to read Revelation 21:1–22:5. What do you think heaven will be like?
5. How can we encourage parents of unfaithful children? What can we do to bring back those who have strayed from God?
6. Name ways Christians can celebrate when their waiting has ended. Have a celebration in class.
7. Why do some people wait to become Christians even after they have learned the truth? Sing the song "Why Do You Wait?" by George F. Root.
8. Have someone tell the parable of the sower. Discuss the different types of soil. What are some ways we can plant the seed?
9. Divide the class into three groups. Ask each group to role-play one of the parables in Luke 15. Discuss what these parables teach.

The Waiting Song

I thank you, Lord, for the joy that comes
  in the midst of the storms of life.
I thank you, Lord, for the shelter
  in the middle of the strife.
I thank you, Lord, for holding me
  in the palm of your hand.
I thank you, Lord, for the water
  in a dry, thirsty land.

My grace is sufficient unto thee,
  my precious child.
Just lean your head on my breast
  and rest a little while.
Your burdens will grow lighter
  with each step of faith you take.
Let me renew your failing strength
  While you learn to wait.

Draw nigh unto me, my child,
  The fears will go away.
I'll hold your hand as we walk
  Along the narrow way.
My arm is not so short
  That I can't do the things you ask.
I'll give you strength and guide you
  to complete every task.

The words of life flow freely
  from his heart unto mine.
I soar like an eagle
  and He's with me all the time.
His blessings, his mercy,
  his goodness follow me.
Oh, Lord, I give you praises
  through all eternity.[1]

—Mary Russell

[1]Russell, Mary. "The Waiting Song." Used by permission of Mary Russell, Booneville, MS. Unpublished.

Bibliography

Barnett, Joe. "Is God Listening?" *UpReach* (Highland Church of Christ, Herald of Truth, Abilene, TX, Nov./Dec. 1984).

Becton, Randy. "The Place of Wonder in the Life of Trust." *UpReach* (Highland Church of Christ, Herald of Truth, Abilene, TX, April/May 1987).

Clarke, Adam. *Clarke's Commentary, vol. IV* (Abingdon-Cokesbury Press, New York, 1810).

Coffey, Tony. "Elijah, Solomon, Apostles Instructed to Wait." *The Christian Chronicle.* (Oklahoma Christian College, Oklahoma City, OK, Aug. 1987).

Doering, Jane. *The Power of Encouragement* (Moody Press, Chicago, IL, 1983).

Hazelip, Harold. "Why Doesn't God Give Me What I Want?", *UpReach* (Highland Church of Christ, Herald of Truth, Abilene, TX, Nov. /Dec. 1984).

Jensen, Amy Hillyard. *Is There Anything I Can Do to Help?* (Pamphlet available from Medic Publishing Co., Redmond, WA, 1980).

Landorf, Joyce (Speaker). "God's Waiting Room" [Cassette Recording]. (Vision House, Inc., Gospel Light Publications, Ventura, CA, 1981).

Landorf, Joyce. "While We Wait." DaySpring Cards. (OutReach Publications, Siloam Springs, AR, 1985).

McMahan, Patricia. "A Legacy for Your Children," *Christian Woman* (Gospel Advocate, Nashville, TN, July/Aug. 1987).

Meir, Paul; Minirth, Frank; Haskins, Don; Flournoy, Richard. *How to Beat Burnout.* (Moody Press, Chicago, IL, 1986).

Michelmore, Peter. "Could They Forgive Their Son's Killer?", *Reader's Digest* (The Reader's Digest Association, Inc., Pleasantville, NY, May, 1986).

Milholland, Sandra Woodroof. "Don't Lose Heart," *UpReach* (Highland Church of Christ, Herald of Truth, Abilene, TX, July/Aug. 1987).

Murray, Andrew. *The Believer's Secret of Waiting on God* (Bethany House Publishers, Minneapolis, MN, 1986).

Rawlinson, George. *The Pulpit Commentary, Isaiah* (Wm. B. Eerdmans Publishing Co., Grand Rapids, MI, 1950).

Richards, Larry. *When It Hurts Too Much to Wait* (Word Books, Waco, TX, 1985).

Russell, Mary. "The Waiting Song." Unpublished.

Sanford, John and Paul. *Restoring the Christian Family* (Logos International, Kansas City, MO, 1979).

Stapp, Phil. "You Were Created to Soar," *UpReach* (Highland Church of Christ, Herald of Truth, Abilene, TX, July/Aug. 1988).

Thompson, Frank Charles, Editor. *The Thompson Chain-Reference Bible, New International Version* (B. B. Kirkbride Bible Co., Inc., Indianapolis, IN, and Zondervan Bible Publishers, Grand Rapids, MI, 1983).

Thrasher, Bill. "Soar on Wings Like Eagles," *Bulletin Digest* (Jim R. Martin, Publisher, Sesser, IL, Oct./Nov. 1988).

Watt, Leilani. *Caught in the Conflict* (Harvest House Publishers, Eugene, OR, 1984).